LINCOLN CHRISTIAN COLLEGE   P9-CFZ-180

"This honest book is invaluable for worship planners who desire to develop a common vocabulary allowing them to investigate the perils and possibilities of using media art in the worship of their faith community. Dr. Crowley convinced me to keep reading when she wrote, '. . . the use of media [in worship] can be suspect when media draws disproportionate attention to the worshipers, the performers, or the art, rather than to the holy One who is the Creator and to God's creation-in-need' and 'people should be the starting point, not technology.'"

Scott Weidler
Associate Director for Worship & Music
Evangelical Lutheran Church in America

"Crowley provides a practical, clearly written resource for worship leaders now studying, or already embracing, the use of electronic and digital multimedia resources in preaching and liturgy. Her book is an affirmation and celebration of new forms of liturgical media art now made possible with inexpensive and widely available new media technology, while offering clear evaluative frameworks to guide worship leaders and teams in their creative and collaborative work.

"After providing a common vocabulary sure to help practitioners understand and talk about the nature of their work clearly, Crowley then moves us into a balanced discussion about the theological and artistic challenges and opportunities in today's digital communication milieu, looking to the guidance of past and present Catholic and Protestant discussion and practice, as well as current new media theory. This book is a must-read for clergy and laity considering or already developing locally produced liturgical media art."

Michael Bausch
author of *Silver Screen, Sacred Story:*
Using Multimedia in Worship (The Alban Institute, 2002)
and director of www.worshipmedia.com

"The emergence of new artistic forms in liturgy offers us the opportunity not only to explore new territory but also to test the criteria by which we judge all art forms. The accessibility of this volume promises to stimulate instructive discussions of these criteria in local worshiping communities, as well as to help local artists of all kinds imagine new ways that they can contribute to vital, faithful worship. The best local discussions of this topic should follow Eileen Crowley's own approach of drawing on liturgical, theological, and technical expertise."

> John D. Witvliet
> Calvin Institute of Christian Worship
> Calvin College and Calvin Theological Seminary
> Grand Rapids, Michigan

"This little book is a masterful introduction to media in worship, its historical and cultural context, and its possibilities and perils. Drawing on her professional experience as media producer and liturgist, Eileen Crowley lays out four very helpful frameworks for discerning whether, how, and what media to incorporate in worship, and she proposes a community-based model for developing such media. Her primary concern throughout is for the liturgy itself and for the people who cele-brate it. No matter where one stands on media in worship—practitioner, opponent, or undecided—Crowley has provided a timely and much needed reflective guide that will surely advance both discussion and liturgical practice. A must-read for thinking about liturgical art in a media culture!"

> Gilbert Ostdiek, O.F.M.
> Professor of Liturgy
> Catholic Theological Union
> Chicago, Illinois

AMERICAN ESSAYS IN LITURGY

Series Editor, Edward Foley

Liturgical Art
for a Media Culture

Eileen D. Crowley

LITURGICAL PRESS
Collegeville, Minnesota

www.litpress.org

Scripture is from the New Revised Standard Version Bible, copyright 1989, Division of Christian Education of the National Council of the Churches of Christ in the United States of America. Used by permission. All rights reserved.

© 2007 by Order of Saint Benedict, Collegeville, Minnesota. All rights reserved. No part of this book may be reproduced in any form, by print, microfilm, microfiche, mechanical recording, photocopying, translation, or by any other means, known or yet unknown, for any purpose except brief quotations in reviews, without the previous written permission of Liturgical Press, Saint John's Abbey, P.O. Box 7500, Collegeville, Minnesota 56321-7500. Printed in the United States of America.

1   2   3   4   5   6   7   8   9

Library of Congress Cataloging-in-Publication Data

Crowley, Eileen D.
    Liturgical art for a media culture / Eileen D. Crowley.
       p. cm. — (American essays in liturgy)
    ISBN 978-0-8146-2968-0
    1. Public worship—Audio-visual aids.   2. Liturgy and the arts.
    3. Liturgics.   4. Mass media—Religious aspects—Christianity.   I. Title.

BV288.C76 2007
264.0028—dc22   2006035392

Contents

5-19

118101

101811

Introduction

Media and Worship in Today's Media Cultures

Nearly three decades after the bishops of the Second Vatican Council released their Decree on the Means of Social Communications (*Inter Mirifica*, 1963)—a document that referred to media as "marvellous technical inventions"[1]—the Pontifical Council on Social Communication published a pastoral letter about insights since gained. This pastoral letter proclaimed the end of the twentieth century to be the Dawn of a New Era (*Aetatis Novae*, 1992) in the church's relationship with media arts and technologies, and with those who produce, use, and encounter them:

> Today, much that men and women know and think about is conditioned by the media; to a considerable extent, human experience itself is an experience of media. . . . The use of new media gives rise to what some speak of as "new languages" and has given birth to new possibilities for the mission of the Church as well as to new pastoral problems.[2]

Projected photographs, computer graphics, feature film clips, video stories, animation, and combinations of these are among the "new media" that have entered Christian worship. These media truly do present new opportunities, as well as new "pastoral problems." During the last three decades, and since the 1990s in particular, churches Protestant and Catholic have taken up the challenge of how to use this "new language" in their praise and thanks, as well as in their confession, supplication, and lamentation.

Media technologies, "both mass and interpersonal, are deeply embedded in our lives," notes media scholar Michael A. Real. In what he calls this "media culture," these technologies "interact abundantly with each other."[3] Media culture flourishes in homes, schools, and workplaces, as well as in commercial, institutional, and public spaces. That media technologies have increasingly entered Christian worship spaces, then, is no surprise: Worshipers naturally swim in the media culture ocean that is their everyday habitat.

Historically speaking, the recent incorporation of media can be seen in continuity with the centuries-long pattern of Christians appropriating the aural and visual media of their day for the glory of God and for the spiritual benefit and uplifting of the assembled faithful. To see better the correlation and connections over time, one need only take a slightly different perspective and view worship itself as a complex, multifaceted communal performance. Before any of today's new media enters a sanctuary or church auditorium, worship is already a multi-sensory, multi-art, multimedia event. Over the centuries worship has involved, to one degree or another, ritual speech, music, visual arts, lighting, dress, movement, gestures, posture, tastes, and fragrances. Adding today's new media to these old media does not make worship multimedia. Liturgy has always been multimedia.[4]

Typically, the introduction of new media into worship over the last century has been for the sake of better communications, evangelism, or increased congregational participation, not for the creation of liturgical art. Robb Redman points to media's supporting role in what he calls The Great Worship Awakening of the second half of the twentieth century. He traces the origins of the Great Worship Awakening to major movements in Christian worship: the praise and worship movement begun in the 1950s, the ecumenical liturgical renewal movement with official major worship reforms starting in the 1960s, and the seeker service movement inaugurated in the late 1970s. He suggests the development of the contemporary worship music industry as another major contributor to this Awakening. Since the 1950s, it is important to note, the introduction of these new forms of worship and new kinds of worship music have gone hand-in-hand with the employment of new forms of media technologies and arts as churches have sought ways to revitalize their worship.[5] Since the 1970s in particular, media technologies and new media have gradually become an integral, even an expected element of worship in many nondenominational and denominational churches. For a still relatively small but growing number of faith communities in diverse places around the world—Australia, Brazil, Canada, Dominican Republic, England, Germany, Indonesia, New Zealand, Northern Ireland, Scotland, Singapore, South Korea, Taiwan, the United States, and Wales—media in worship has become the norm for Sunday worship. In the United States alone, by one estimate, two thousand churches adopt some form of media each year.[6]

The combination of media technologies and arts incorporated into church services varies from one church space to another and from one worship and ecclesial context to another. Pastors have added new media not only to Sunday worship but also to funerals, weddings, evening prayer, Good Friday liturgies, reconciliation services, youth-oriented worship, and other services. Many worshipers have appreciated these innovations.

Growth-oriented churches, including those referred to as megachurches, have been leaders in actively promoting the use of a variety of media technologies and arts to convey the Good News to the unchurched. Their media ministers have produced and provided media resources for their own use and for other churches' use, as well. They have written "how-to" books and have offered workshops, conferences, and consultation services to other churches whose leaders have adopted or are considering adopting media as an element in their worship. For those in communities, denominations, and countries where media has not yet entered the worship of local churches, this worship development might seem startling, as if it were something suddenly erupting on the worship landscape. Since the mid-twentieth century, though, multiple factors have contributed to the escalating incorporation of media alongside other communications technologies and arts. During the last decade in particular, decreased costs of media technologies and software and increased accessibility of media production and projection equipment have brought the possibility of media in worship within the reach of even very small churches.

Nonprofit and for-profit groups offering media-for-worship products and services to churches have created a mini-industry. Suppliers, consultants, and products can be easily found through Internet searches, trade and church magazines, and church-related conferences.

Because the focus of church leaders and worship media industry leaders has been primarily on improving communication, what has yet to emerge is an appreciation of new media's potential to give birth to liturgical art. Media technologies, graphics packages, and editing software may be used artfully and artistically in the production of media for worship, but their product is not typically considered art, and their creators do not typically consider themselves artists.

Media in worship does present new opportunities and new problems. As a liturgist and media producer myself, I contend that the creative, imaginative, and skillful use of media technologies and arts has the potential to produce a new form of liturgical art and, with it, a new liturgical ministry. As with all liturgical arts, though, the use of this art ideally involves thoughtful, prayerful discernment that takes into account questions of community, liturgy, aesthetics, and ethics.

While some church leaders have enthusiastically embraced media for their community's worship, other church leaders have rejected outright the use of media technologies (except, typically, audio amplification) and media arts, claiming they are never appropriate for worship. This essay is designed to prompt further reflection for both sides of that spectrum of opinion, and it will also guide the reflection of all those Christians in between who wonder what doing worship in a media culture might mean for their faith communities.

This evolving media ministry is still at a very basic level of development. In ways comparable to folk music introduced in worship in the United States in the 1960s and 1970s, media in worship might be said to be at the "three-chord stage" of artistic, liturgical, and technical development. Yet even at this early stage, media technologies and arts are already affecting worship in the United States and elsewhere, and this development deserves pastoral attention and theological reflection.

To assist church leaders and members in assessing the possibilities and problems associated with media in worship, the following chapters will provide a basic introduction to this topic: chapter 1, a vocabulary for constructive church dialogue and discernment; chapter 2, a historical overview of this worship phenomenon; chapter 3, an assessment of perils and positive possibilities; chapter 4, four critical frameworks for communities' discernment of their own media in worship; and chapter 5, a new model for this liturgical ministry: Communal Co-Creation.

Notes

1. *Inter Mirifica*, no. 1, December 4, 1963. Translation of phrase from *Vatican II: The Basic Sixteen Documents*, ed. Austin Flannery, rev. ed. (Northport, NY: Costello Publishing, 1996), 539.

2. *Aetatis Novae* (The Dawn of a New Era), no. 2, Pontifical Council on Social Communications, February 22, 1992.

3. Michael A. Real, *Exploring Media Culture: A Guide* (Thousand Oaks, CA: Sage Publications, 1996), 6.

4. The term "media" in art history previously had been restricted to the medium used in the creation of a work of art, e.g., paint, stone, glass, metal, sound, bodies. In twentieth-century common usage, "media" has become synonymous with electronically or digitally produced and transmitted mass media, small group media, and interpersonal communications media.

5. Robb Redman, *The Great Worship Awakening: Singing a New Song in the Postmodern Church* (San Francisco: Jossey-Bass, 2002).

6. Mark Manley, "New Tools for Worship Presentations," *Technologies for Worship Magazine* (May/June 1999): 19.

1 A Working Vocabulary for Church Dialogue and Discernment

It is not uncommon for church discussion about media in worship to degenerate into polemics or into debates based on personal media preferences and tastes. Such conflict is not surprising. Church leaders and members include both media-philes and media-phobes. They see media, in general, from different perspectives. They may have radically differing views and expectations of worship as well. Thus, media in worship can be a volatile subject that ignites passionate debate. Churches need a productive, constructive way to address the issues related to this phenomenon. Ideally, participants in any discussion need to commit themselves to dialogue marked by charity, openness, and genuine listening. If mutually respectful and fruitful reflection is to occur, it is best if participants begin from a common point of departure.

For a start, it is helpful for all those engaged in such conversations to use vocabulary that is mutually understood. True dialogue requires that those attempting to speak and to listen actually have a chance of communicating with each other. To allow all points of view to be adequately and clearly communicated, we need a common working vocabulary related to this phenomenon of media in worship. Careful use of media in worship also requires a vocabulary in which distinctions are carefully made. The following vocabulary can provide such a common ground and starting point for a worshiping community's discussion and informed critical reflection.

Terms associated with worship

Worship includes the full range of individual and communal praise and thanksgiving, confession and supplication, adoration and lamentation. This general term can apply to ritual practices of adherents of many religions.[1] A general term, this word often is used synonymously for "liturgy," although the latter term can be more narrowly defined.

Liturgy emphasizes the communal aspect of worship, since this word's origin comes from the Greek *leitourgia*, typically translated as "the work of the people."[2] Liturgy often signifies worship that involves a particular order of actions in religious rituals, a particular worship tradition, or a new arrangement of ritual actions developed to fulfill a particular communal need.[3] As used in this book, liturgy is further understood to be ritual that assumes the active participation of those present, including active contemplation. It is ritual in which the participants ideally understand themselves as actors and not as audience members. Those who participate in liturgy eventually come to realize, in part because of the modeling behavior of regular congregants, that they are expected to perform ritual actions such as singing, reciting prayers, taking part in confessions and ritual responses, listening attentively, or moving in ritual ways. Liturgy, following this participation model, then, is different from seeker-oriented or any other services that, for evangelism purposes, follow a performance model. In such services, those who attend are treated as welcomed guests. They are invited to watch and to listen to the on-stage action of preachers, musicians, actors, or others who perform, and to experience media produced to help communicate the church's message; but they usually are not expected to contribute in any other way, including monetarily.

Liturgical art signifies any form of art that is integral and appropriate to the liturgical actions of a community's liturgy. The context and function of this art differentiates it from other forms of art.[4] A distinct form of art, liturgical art is wedded to liturgical action and/or a liturgical environment.[5]

Terms associated with art and artists in general

Art is a general term that can encompass the processes and products of a person or group of persons who intentionally and imaginatively use expressive media of any sort to produce an artifact or an experience for the use, benefit, contemplation, inspiration, or interaction of others. Art is a social practice.[6] It involves communal standards, expectations, skills, and traditions. Art is not necessarily only what some might see as high art. It includes folk art, tribal art, popular art, graphic art, and even what have been called crafts. It involves human creation of some thing, some performance, or some experience that draws those who encounter it into a dialogue because art requires their active interpretation and participation. Art is designed to communicate and, ideally, to move those who experience it emotionally, spiritually, intellectually, even physically. It operates on multiple levels at the same time.

Artist refers to individuals or to a collaborative group who "perceive, order, clarify, intensify, and interpret a certain aspect of the human condition for themselves" and for others.[7]

Media art refers to artistically created products or experiences that can result from any combination of electric, electronic, or digital technologies. This art can often be found combined with other art forms such as prose or poetry, music or other artistically generated sound, two-dimensional visual art (e.g., painting, photography, computer art), three-dimensional art (e.g., furnishings, sculpture, installation art, or an architectural space), kinetic art (e.g., cinematography or video art), or performance arts (e.g., drama, dance, mime). Media art is a hybrid art.

Terms associated with media in general

Media, in the twenty-first century technological sense, is a commonplace term that refers to hardware and software systems and to the products of those media technologies.[8]

Multimedia is commonly used in a broad sense to refer to multiple forms of arts and communications working together to create an experience. In the narrower technological sense, this term has evolved in meaning, especially since the 1960s when it denoted a large screen or multi-screen, multi-image event. In the 1990s people began to use this term to refer to media products displayed on a single computer monitor.[9] In this essay the term multimedia refers broadly to the artistic combination of multiple media technologies that creates an overall, multisensory experience for a group of people. This term includes, in effect, its older and newer connotations.

Video is another general term people commonly use to speak about media art of any kind, whether produced by professionals or amateurs, that is projected through video technology onto a computer screen, video projection screen, television monitor, wall, fabric, or other surface. Consequently, video means much more than the products of the mass media entertainment industry (e.g., TV programs and movies), although people may use this term in reference to such products.

Terms associated with media used in worship

Media in worship refers to media systems and products used in worship, regardless of how they are employed. Media in worship can comprise any combination of nineteenth- and twentieth-century media forms: photography; cinematography; overhead projectors and transparencies; multimedia presentations with multiple active screens and audio tracks; audio recording and playback technologies including magnetic tape, CD, CD-ROM, DVD; music and computer-related forms of music and other sounds; video technologies, cameras, games, and video art; computer technologies and computer art; integrative digital multimedia technologies and digital art; and interactive performance and installation arts. All of these technologies and art forms can potentially be put to the service of a community's worship.

Media in worship, as addressed in this essay, includes what is created, as well as what is purchased or appropriated for worship. Churches can now license or buy, often through Internet Web sites, worship-related media art and complete media packages that are frequently designed to be customized by the local church. Media available to worship leaders include: Scripture-based, lectionary-based, and theme-based graphics and video; background photographs, animations, and video; feature film and documentary clips; video vignettes; lyrics; Scripture-of the-day text; and unison and responsive prayers.

Liturgical media art distinguishes media art that is integral to the actions of a community's liturgy, that is, media art *of* the liturgy, as opposed to media simply being used *in* liturgy.

Liturgical media artists are liturgical ministers who, regardless of their skill level or compensation (or lack thereof), create some form of liturgical art or environment that involves the use of media.

Equipped with a common vocabulary, church leaders, church members, liturgists, theologians, and seminarians may have less difficulty understanding each other's view points when discussing media in worship. Discussions would also be aided if participants came to the table with some historical context, a matter the following chapter will address.

Notes

1. "Worship is a universal phenomenon. It consists in a response of veneration in the face of the recognized presence of God . . . (and) may be private or even individualistic." Patrick Bishop, "Worship," in *The New Dictionary of Sacramental Worship,* ed. Peter E. Fink (Collegeville, MN: Liturgical Press, 1990), 1331–32.

2. Catholic theology from the Second Vatican Council holds that "the liturgy, then, is rightly seen as the priestly office of Jesus Christ" and only derivatively the work of the people in so far as the whole public worship "is performed by the Mystical Body of Jesus Christ, that is, by the Head and his members." *Sacrosanctum Concilium* (The Constitution on the Sacred Liturgy), no. 7, in *Vatican II: The Basic Sixteen Documents,* 121.

3. "The amount and kind of Christian prayer that has been referred to by the term liturgy has varied over time." Today the term, as understood in Catholicism, for example, refers to the rites contained in officially promulgated ritual books, including the rites for the seven sacraments, the dying, Christian burial, dedication of a church, religious profession, installation of liturgical ministers, morning and evening prayer, and blessings. It is "distinguished from private prayer and from other pious exercises." Lawrence J. Madden, "Liturgy," in *The New Dictionary of Sacramental Worship,* ed. Peter E. Fink (Collegeville, MN: Liturgical Press, 1990), 742–44.

4. Joseph Gelineau created a taxonomy to describe the differences among liturgical, religious, and sacred music. Gelineau's taxonomy for *music,* I suggest, can be applied to distinguish liturgical, religious, and sacred *art.* In doing so, the broadest category of art, *religious art,* would include art that may have a religious theme or "expresses a religious sentiment but is not designated for use in the liturgy." *Sacred art* would be more narrowly defined, since "by its inspiration, purpose, and destination or manner of use [it] has a connection with the faithful." Over time, this art has become accepted as something sa-

16

cred to believers. Given the liturgical reforms of the 1960s, *liturgical art* would be art *of* the liturgy, rather than art performed or simply located *in* a worship space. Gelineau's taxonomy cited in Edward Foley, "Liturgical Music," *The New Dictionary of Sacramental Worship*, ed. Peter E. Fink (Collegeville, MN: Liturgical Press, 1990), 855.

5. G. Thomas Ryan, *The Sacristy Manual* (Chicago, IL: Liturgy Training Publications, 1993), 22.

6. "A practice is a socially embodied way of doing something, such that there are not only correct and incorrect, and effective and ineffective ways of doing it, but better and worse ways. Social practices provide us with ways of achieving excellence which, apart from those practices, simply don't exist." Nicholas Wolterstorff, "Two Ways of Thinking About Art: Part I and II" in *K–12 Education: Culture and Community* (Grand Rapids, MI: The Van Andel Educational Institute, 2000), 47–48.

7. Herbert Zettl, *Sight Sound Motion: Applied Media Aesthetics*, 3rd ed. (Belmont: Wadsworth Publishing, 1999), 4. Artists, George Steiner writes, are interpreters of Real Presence: "All serious art, music and literature is a *critical act*" that embodies "concentrated, selective interactions between the constraints of the observed and the boundless possibilities of the imagined." George Steiner, *Real Presences* (Chicago, IL: University of Chicago Press, 1989), 11.

8. Within the context of worship, this word does not refer to mass media or to the different materials artists might use (e.g., paint, wood, metal) in creating their art.

9. With the introduction of the Kodak Cavalcade™ and Kodak Carousel™ projectors in the 1960s, multimedia as a term referred to an installation of rapidly changing images projected or displayed on an arrangement of multiple slide screens or video monitors, with the projection of related or unrelated images synchronized in some fashion with music, narration, or some other soundtrack. More recently, the term, and that to which it refers, has shrunk in the spatial dimensions implied. This word now is often limited to meaning any kind of audio-visual presentation that is displayed on a computer monitor, such as a video game, website, or instructional program. John K. Larish, "Multimedia," in *Focal Encyclopedia of Photography*, ed. Leslie Stroebel and Richard Zakia, 3rd ed. (Boston, MA: Focal Press, 1993), 497.

2 A History of Media in Christian Worship in the United States

At a picnic one summer's day, a conversation about media in worship triggered a neighbor of mine to offer an anecdote about her one and only experience of this phenomenon. Many years after having moved away from her former Episcopal parish, she explained, she returned there to participate in a special liturgy. Bussed in from many surrounding parishes, people were packed into the historic colonial-period church in Northern Virginia. My neighbor managed to find a seat in this worship space, a place that she had always loved. The service began. Just before the congregation was about to sing, a media screen suddenly rolled down from the sanctuary ceiling. "I was so startled," she recalled. "It seemed so intrusive. But I guess they must have needed it." She tried to think of a reason, and came up with this: "Maybe because we might not all know the same songs. . . . But it sure was ugly."

This vignette offers a glimpse of how unexpected and unsettling media in worship can still be for some worshipers in the United States, even at the start of the twenty-first century. This chapter's task is to explain how this innovation entered North American Christian worship.

Projecting the Glory:
Foundations for Worship Experiments, 1910–1925

The projection of images, texts, and other audiovisual products in worship today has grown from the roots of nineteenth- and twentieth-century innovations in projection equipment, photography, and cinematography, as well as from advances in other forms of art and technology.

In the nineteenth century, popular audiences enjoyed the wonders of projections using different techniques and showing various kinds of content: magic lantern shows, phantasmagorias, peepshows, panoramas, and dioramas. Starting in the early eighteen hundreds, magic lantern shows of projected hand-drawn and hand-painted images provided "a form of traveling entertainment."[1] By mid-century, projections in private and public spaces included images photographically produced. With the advent of slide photography and slide-changing mechanisms in the late 1800s, this popular entertainment took on new configurations. Presenters could stack multiple magic lantern projectors to create an early form of a multimedia-style show through photographic superimposition.[2] Other inventions—including George Eastman's first commercial transparent roll film (1889) and Thomas Edison's motion picture camera and projector (1891)—ultimately gave birth to a twentieth-century boom in amateur photography and the birth of the commercial movie industry. Moving pictures created the illusion of motion. Viewers found them moving.[3]

In *The Silents of God: Selected Issues and Documents in Silent American Film and Religion 1908–1925*, media historian Terry Lindvall provides invaluable information on the early history of media in worship. "Congregationalists formed . . . the apologetic vanguard in making a case for motion pictures" in their ministry, he reports.[4] When Congregational ministers in the 1910s started showing stereopticon slides and silent movie reels with religious themes as part of their services, media art in worship was a radical worship innovation.[5] In addition to their showing silent movies as wholesome amusement for families and as educational tools, pastors also used them to illustrate sermons "where formerly the stereopticon was used," according to George J. Anderson. In his report to fellow ministers, Anderson notes the example of Congregational and Presbyterian churches in Redlands, California, holding summer Sunday evening services in an outdoor movie pavilion, services in which preachers used "moving pictures of a religious nature."[6] City and country churches purchased movie projectors for use in lectures, religious education, and evangelization efforts to reach the unchurched and immigrants. While most churches at this time had reportedly not embraced the use of silent movies for their Sunday services, religious revivalists understood film's value in drawing crowds.[7]

Lindvall offers voices from clergy who advocated silent movies in worship. In 1912 Rev. E. Boudinot Stockton reported in the trade journal, *Moving Picture World,* on experiments using film in "religious and devotional services as distinct from their employment as a means of sacred and semi-sacred amusement and recreation suitable for Sunday." Stockton quotes a letter in which Rev. Edgar Fay Daugherty, minister of the First Christian Church of Vincennes, Indiana, describes his use of film in Sunday evening services. At the start of one service, "lantern slides shown on the screen" accompanied an organ and choral rendition of "the sacred song, 'The Way of the Cross.'" After a responsive reading and a prayer, twelve slides illustrated a choir and congregational hymn, "Work for the Night is Coming." A short movie, *An Innocent Theft,* the collection, and "a short lesson on the moral taught by the moving picture" followed. Five slides illustrated another song, "Throw Out the Life Line," after which "the service concluded with the benediction and an organ postlude."[8]

Stockton heartily endorsed Daugherty's liturgical approach and suggested that this kind of service order would be possible for worship in other Christian churches, both Protestant and Catholic.[9] Stockton further suggested that, for mission services and other worship occasions, stereopticon slides worked well for texts and congregational lyrics: "Instead of pictures the lantern threw on the screen the words of the hymn or psalm or portion of Scripture wished and the minister and congregation sang or read from the screen. On two occasions the music as well as the words of unknown hymns were projected and the children were taught to sing. "[10]

Obviously, not all were as eager as the Reverends Stockton and Daugherty to imagine how still and motion pictures could add new dimensions to worship. However, throughout the 1910s, forward-thinking churches across the United States adopted moving pictures for education, inspiration, evangelization, and entertainment. A report in 1920 estimated that some 2,000 churches, Protestant and Catholic, were then employing motion pictures.[11] The Community Motion Picture Bureau of New York built a library of more than 2,000 reels specifically selected to serve churches.[12]

At the start of the 1920s, some Methodists had joined the Congregationalists in their efforts to bring the movie into the pulpit; other denominations tapped the movies' potential for evangelization, education, or the Americanization of immigrants.[13] Churches were making such extensive use of movies to attract crowds that some movie theater owners grew concerned about a potential decline in their customers.[14] What Lindvall calls The Great Divorce solved that problem.[15]

From 1921 to 1923, scandals in the movie industry diminished the potential for the movies to serve as "handmaiden" to religion.[16] Dramatic sex comedies appalled some church leaders, and restrictive Blue Laws closed theaters on Sunday.[17] Advocates of church use of moving pictures found themselves on the defensive. Hollywood began to treat as taboo the making of movies with a religious theme.[18] Movie distributors started to refuse to rent movies to churches.[19] The decade-long partnership between the expanding movie industry and the Christian churches of the United States gradually split apart.[20] During this period in the United States, a battle for Christianity itself was being played out on the Protestant evangelical landscape, a battle between liberals and conservatives. The relationship of religion to popular culture, such as moving pictures, became one of the battlegrounds.[21] Not until the 1950s did ministers once more see the potential for contemporary audiovisual media to serve as "the handmaiden" of worship.

Media Re-enters Worship, 1950–1970s

Post-World War II trends in technology, worship, evangelism, and art dominate the media-in-worship history of the 1950s–1970s. To understand the current twenty-first-century worship phenomenon and media's widespread acceptance in church services, one needs to appreciate the significance of these trends. Like tributaries they have converged and interacted. They have produced a rapid river of media technology and arts that has naturally flowed into Christian worship in North America and elsewhere. The most obvious trend, and the easiest to track, involves advances and innovations in technology. Two specifically church-related trends emerging in the 1950s arise from efforts toward renewal of Catholic and Protestant worship and from new methods of evangelization. In the 1960s, artists and critics inside the world of institutional art create and witness the fourth trend. This artistic trend included major changes in attitudes and practice: the blurring of the boundaries between "high" and "popular" art and between art and everyday life; the decisions of individual artists to work with media technologies to produce new kinds of art; and the growing public acceptance of diverse forms of media beyond the mass media of TV and radio.

Technology

The technology trend includes advances in photography and in image projection. Mid-century advances built upon the solid technological and photographic foundations of nineteenth- and early twentieth-century innovations. From the 1920s onward, making images and projecting them became more and more affordable and certainly less cumbersome, even for amateurs. Among new options for amateurs were 16mm and 8mm movie film, cameras, and projection technology; 35mm still cameras using new slide transparency film; single-lens reflex cameras (SLRs); and 35mm cardboard slide mounts. In the film industry, directors took advantage of new artistic opportunities with the advent of feature-length motion picture film (a decided advance over the limits of the ten-minute reels of silent movies) and sound for those films.[22] Of particular interest for the media-in-worship story is the introduction of three different kinds of projection systems introduced in the 1940s and 1950s: the overhead projector with its write-on transparent sheets; the 16mm color filmstrip and projector; and the Kodak Cavalcade™ Projector, the first fully automatic color slide projector. In the following decades, these projection systems eventually found their way into the religious education wings of most Protestant churches and into the classrooms of Catholic parochial schools.

In the 1950s Protestant preachers in evangelical and Baptist churches could roll in an overhead projector, instead of a chalkboard, to literally magnify their sermon points for their listeners.[23] In the mid-1950s, one Catholic seminary in Missouri was using projection equipment for the presentation of lyrics and musical notation to help students chant Latin Mass propers and to sing English hymns.[24]

In some instances, Assemblies of God pastors not only projected lyrics for congregational singing but also would bring in television equipment to show, as part of their service, sermons by the evangelical televangelist Jimmy Swaggart.[25] Once video monitors came into the sanctuary, pastors could use television graphics to support their sermons, along with slides and film clips. Not too far behind the Pentecostals, the Baptists continued to increase their use of media, and some began to broadcast their services. However, based on anecdotal evidence from those who ministered and worshiped in the late 1960s and early 1970s, such expansion of the use of media was rare.

Worship

New forms of worship began to take advantage of these projection technologies. The Charismatic Renewal Movement of the 1960s fostered a participation model for worship, a form of worship energized by numerous praise choruses. In developing what have since come to be called praise and worship services, Pentecostal churches such as the Assemblies of God found that projected lyrics freed congregants from holding hymnals and gave them an option to express bodily their experience of the Spirit. Projected lyrics also allowed leaders to introduce the latest congregational songs.[26] With the introduction of official Catholic liturgical reforms after the Second Vatican Council, leaders in Catholic churches, colleges, and high schools experimented with projecting slides as media for meditation during different moments in liturgies.[27] Some Protestant leaders, alarmed with declining worship attendance, also sought to renew their worship and to make it more relevant for the TV generation. They did so by experimenting with projected slides, overhead transparencies, and short films.[28] One movie, *The Parable*, fit easily into the order of mainline Protestant services. This fifteen-minute film that featured a Christ-figure clown was controversial when first shown at the Protestant-Orthodox pavilion at the 1964 World's Fair for which it was originally created. Afterward, it circulated widely among mainline Protestant churches, and in many churches this film likely was the first movie most worshipers had ever seen in their service.[29]

During this period individual churches occasionally inserted media into their worship, basically for communications purposes. Churches tended to use media in ways similar to how it was then being used in schools and businesses. Protestant ministers found that audiovisual technology could help them project sermon points or illustrations, encourage congregational singing, or invite worshipers to prayer. Even at this early stage of acceptance, though, Catholic and Protestant leaders demonstrated different attitudes toward the use of visuals in worship. They may have used the same projection equipment, but they tended to use them differently. Consider two cases from the 1970s.

With the introduction of liturgical reforms in the Catholic Church from the mid-1960s through the 1970s, liturgical leaders in the United States and elsewhere became engaged in a transitional phase that permitted a certain level of officially sanctioned local experimentation in worship. One of the places where such experimentation occurred weekly was in the "media chapel" of Liturgy in Santa Fe, the worship of an intentional community of Catholics. Its liturgical leaders developed the use of media art as just one art among others integral to their worship. This decade-long experiment began in 1970 in Santa Fe, New Mexico. There, Dominican Blase Schauer, local artists, and other parishioners used a variety of arts for every liturgy, including even the culinary arts for theme-oriented, post-worship community feasts. Local photographers provided their own slides to support scriptural, liturgical, or seasonal themes. Art teachers, art historians, artists, and other volunteers found and copied religious imagery for what ultimately might become a post-communion series of projected images or a single slide whose image served as a subtle visual announcement of the feast. Calligraphers contributed their skills in making works of beauty of mass prayer texts and lyric-and-musical notation. Their carefully designed texts, reminiscent of medieval illuminated manuscripts, were then photographed and transformed into slides for projection during worship. Still other parishioners gathered and displayed borrowed museum and local artists' work in a gallery-like gathering space that led to the chapel. Before worshipers even entered the sanctuary, the art they encountered set a liturgical spirit, tone, mood, and color. This multi-art, multimedia approach to liturgy reflected an implicit, enacted theology of art, one that included media art as a legitimate art form. The way this community incorporated the arts was in continuity with one strand of Catholic tradition's welcoming of a variety of liturgical arts as potential media of God's revelation. In this worship space of "illuminated walls," the artful use of projected slides—along with careful use of sound and silence—went far beyond the utilitarian. Media in Liturgy in Santa Fe was truly a form of liturgical art.[30]

Liturgy in Santa Fe came to an end at the close of the 1970s after the community had to relocate its worship location several times and, ultimately, Father Schauer relocated, as well. During that decade, though, this community's multimedia approach to liturgy and that of other Catholic churches' experimentation demonstrated the possibilities for this medium as liturgical art. In 1978 a major document on liturgical art and environment from the National Conference of Catholic Bishops' Committee on the Liturgy did include three short articles pertaining to audiovisual media and to its appropriate use in worship. For the few liturgical leaders who wanted to experiment with this media art, at least these closing guidelines in *Environment and Art in Catholic Worship* testified to the possibility and legitimacy of this art form, as well as the uncertainty of its future directions:

> It is too early to predict the effect of contemporary audiovisual media—films, videotape, records, tapes—on the public worship of Christians. It is safe to say that a new church building or renovation project should make provision for screens and/or walls which will make the projection of films, slides, and filmstrips visible to the entire assembly, as well as an audio system capable for fine electronic reproduction of sound.[31]

Despite that official acknowledgment of media, liturgical media art became only an occasional element in Catholic worship in the United States.

Evangelization

In contrast to Liturgy in Santa Fe's experiment that used media for liturgical renewal, media was used elsewhere in the late 1970s as a tool for evangelization in a new form of worship designed to attract the unchurched. Nondenominational evangelical pastor Bill Hybels took what he had learned in reaching out to unchurched teens and applied it to reaching out to unchurched baby boomers. He and his team of volunteers and staff created innovative seeker services that depended heavily on popular music, drama, and multimedia to support what was—and still is to this day—basically a Sunday preaching service. In the late 1970s, Hybels' youthful media team produced slide and audio segments to set the theme for a service, to support a sermon, or to provide a visual background for a drama. Started in the Willow Creek Movie Theater, the seeker service "programming" approach to attracting nonbelievers incorporated projected media predominantly for presentation purposes.[32] The media team worked with different multimedia genres. An edited audio and slide "man-on-the-street" interview segment might begin a service. A series of photographs accompanying a popular song might be used to set a theme. Still images might also serve as background in place of a stage set for a drama, a creative performance art that was also an integral element in the Willow Creek programming approach. The growing Willow Creek Church continually invested in better sound, media, and lighting equipment. "Having long recognized people's deep indifference to typical church services, Hybels committed half of his church's meager weekly offerings to pay for multimedia to feature in the services."[33]

Other evangelical and mainline Protestant churches whose leaders were less committed to investment in multimedia eventually did switch from overhead projectors to Kodak Carousel™ projectors for their projected lyrics and sermon support. Some preachers occasionally used 16mm film clips. If they used media at all, though, into the 1970s most churches were still solidly slide-oriented, a nineteenth-century technology actually. However, Willow Creek and other growth-oriented churches that became known as megachurches, such as Saddleback Valley Church in California and Community Church of Joy in Arizona, invested in and adopted new media technologies as they became more affordable. As Douglas C. Mohrmann explains, "The availability of low-cost, high quality technology and an emphasis on the visual arts has translated into an advertising strategy that . . . separated megachurches from other churches."[34] From its introduction in the 1970s, the megachurch media-in-worship approach steadily became *the* model for many growth-oriented Protestant churches, nondenominational as well as denominational.

Art

Meanwhile, in their use of media, United States churches lagged far behind the art world whose artists had been moving media in other directions since the 1960s. Through pop art and other new approaches to art-making, artists such as Andy Warhol challenged the hegemony of the institutionally defined idea of art as "high art" and intentionally blurred the boundaries between art and the everyday. Some artists turned to communications and computer technology to create new forms of art. A "cross-fertilization of arts" contributed to the 1960s creativity of "performances, happenings and events," notes Michael Rush.[35] Artists delighted in the new possibilities and collaborated with other artists and technicians to create complex media events that stimulated in new ways the people who encountered them.[36] In 1969 a New York gallery owner "opened a show filled with television sets, cameras and video feedback systems and called it, 'TV as a Creative Medium.'" By being shown in a gallery setting, video art joined the other arts as a legitimate art form.[37]

The 1970s was also a time of great technological advances in video and computer technologies and, consequently, of innovation in video-related arts. A new smaller videotape color format, the 3/4-inch video cassette, and the portable cameras that used them, made production outside studios a common option for non-broadcast video production. This new format invigorated video production for institutional and organizational communications. Because it could be produced and distributed on a cassette, video gradually came to replace multimedia as the preferred communications format, except with big events that still required large-screen, spectacular multimedia. This cheaper video technology also made it possible for churches to videotape their services.

Within the United States, the intersecting technological, liturgical, evangelical, and artistic trends of the 1950s through the 1970s did not result in large numbers of churches adopting media in worship. Media in worship became a common feature of large Pentecostal and evangelical Protestant churches. But in medium- and smaller-sized Protestant churches and in Catholic parishes, media equipment and art rarely entered worship.

Growing Acceptance of New Media in Worship, Mid-1980s through Today

The adoption of media for worship arrived without fanfare or denominational encouragement at the grassroots level in mainline

Protestant and Catholic churches. This practice just happened, church by church. From a historical perspective, since the early 1980s the media in worship story has broken into two separate story lines. One media-in-worship approach died out, as the other flourished. The Willow Creek perspective of media—a tool for evangelization—has continued to influence how megachurches have invested in and employed media technology and art in their services. This evangelization tool has, since the mid-1990s, gradually moved beyond large evangelical and Pentecostal churches and entered into the strategic plans of growth-oriented denominational churches.

In contrast, the experimentation with media for liturgical renewal (found in some mainline Protestant and Catholic churches in the 1970s and early 1980s) seems to have died out by the mid-1980s. Only in special settings, such as large youth gatherings or campus ministry worship, did worship leaders continue to appropriate media art and popular media as occasional liturgical elements. Thus, the concept of media as a *liturgical art* did not take hold within mainline Protestant and Catholic liturgical circles. In the late 1970s and 1980s, some other forward-thinking Catholic churches did build projection screens into their architectural designs. That design decision did not mean that media art was thereby a regular element in worship; often projection was used only occasionally.[38] According to liturgical design consultants and architects who worked during that period and who were involved in encouraging media screens, parish leadership changes affected the use of media in worship. Once the liturgical leaders who encouraged the incorporation of media left the parish, those pastors who followed may not have been as enthusiastic or as able to put these screens to work in worship.

As in the previous decades, whenever churches came to depend on media in worship, technological advances often drove the ways in which that media art was used—and how frequently it was used as well. New developments in projection have arguably been the most significant driver. According to media equipment specialists, in the mid-1980s the video projector began to appear in church auditoriums. Media technology vendors who had been marketing media systems to the corporate world began receiving calls from congregational leaders. Churches often used the systems for video magnification of their preachers onto large video screens in their auditoriums. Film maker and former pastor Mel White wrote one of the earliest articles about using video projectors in worship. In 1983 he predicted, "Soon, portable life-size video projections systems will be available for every church."[39] Although White's prediction proved overly optimistic, by the early 1990s his vision was beginning to come true. In regard to evangelical, Baptist, and Methodist churches in northern Florida, for example, one equipment vendor recalls, "In the early 1990s the *leader* churches introduced video projection. Between 1993 and 1995 video projection became accepted by the *average* church."[40] Those churches began to include Catholic churches whose leaders typically adopted media for projection of congregational song lyrics. Another media equipment vendor who operates nationwide reports that, in the mid- to late-1990s, he saw a significant change in the level of interest from both independent and evangelical churches. He started hearing from more and more churches whose leaders wanted to follow the Willow Creek worship model. Dropping equipment prices had made media a possible option for their worship.[41] In short, technological innovations have made the use of media in worship possible, affordable, and desirable.

Church members have also contributed to the growing use of media in worship, not just by their financial contributions, but also by their volunteer efforts. While in the 1990s megachurches hired media professionals to produce their worship media, church leaders also discovered the advantage of enlisting volunteers to help their media staff. Eager amateurs, including young teens, learned to operate video and audio equipment during services and thus freed the staff members to direct the service's overall production. In average-sized churches, the media ministry might more likely consist primarily of such volunteers, guided perhaps by one staff member hired to manage and maintain the media equipment. The creation and introduction into worship of computer-based, fully integrated media systems has meant that media ministers could program cues during the week for whatever media might be required for a Sunday service. With cues thus programmed in advance, volunteers could monitor and operate the media computer screens from central consoles during Sunday worship.

Church volunteers have also made a significant impact on the advancement of graphic arts in worship, this because of their familiarity with graphic design software introduced in the mid-1990s, Microsoft's PowerPoint® program in particular. Using this popular software, volunteer members of church media teams could more easily create graphics for song lyrics. They could also design welcome messages, announcements, unison and responsorial prayers, and sermon points. (Pastors and other non-media staff could, too.) Those designing text images could choose from a wide variety of supplied graphic backgrounds or accompanying images. The use of PowerPoint has been particularly important for small- to medium-sized churches that need to project graphic support for singing or preaching. Many members have been trained outside of church on this software package. Children as early as third grade may learn PowerPoint in school. Business people and educators frequently are quite skilled in its use. The introduction of PowerPoint has meant that congregations, regardless of their size, may have a relatively large talent pool available for recruitment of volunteer graphic artists. Since so many people have the software already loaded on their computers, volunteers can create the graphics at home and not tie up a church computer. In fact, these team members may even bring into worship their own laptop computer and connect it directly to the church's video projector.

Many churches start by using PowerPoint for text slides. Once ministers, their staff, and their media ministry volunteers become comfortable with this software, they often begin to look at other software packages that provide more flexibility: pre-packaged graphic art backgrounds or entire media communications packages for a full year's worth of worship. Some companies are selling software already programmed with Scripture passages and lyrics ready to be easily accessed and projected. Still other companies make convenient and legal the incorporation of feature film clips and professionally produced video vignettes.[42] Furthermore, according to one media equipment vendor, it is not uncommon for churches to graduate from simple PowerPoint/video projector equipment to full-blown, completely integrated media systems in which all media are networked together and can be controlled by just a few people. Some larger churches actually jump into media at that high level. "It doesn't cost $100,000 for a system any more. Projectors in the $4,000 to $10,000 range can do a real nice job. For a church with 500 to 600 people, they might spend about $5,000 to $10,000 for something adequate for worship."[43]

From a worship standpoint, megachurches have been influential in developing the presentation worship model for seeker services. Robb Redman notes:

> The seeker-service strategy burst onto the scene in the 1980s, thanks to the rapid growth of several high-profile megachurches with an iconoclastic and pragmatic approach to Sunday services, including Willow Creek Community Church in suburban Chicago, Saddleback Community Church in southern Orange County [CA], Community Church of Joy near Phoenix, and Ginghamsburg United Methodist Church near Dayton. Their basic principle for designing services was "out with the old and in with the new."[44]

Each of these churches offers workshops, seminars, and conferences on a variety of subjects, including the use of the arts and multimedia. "For seeker churches," Redman explains, "the arts and multimedia technology are not optional extras that add glossy slickness to their services. Rather they are a crucial element of the service because of the way that postmodern, post-Christian North Americans view their world."[45] That view is through media-savvy eyes.

By 1999, according to one company that markets media systems to churches in the United States, church organizations even on a denominational level had embraced technological enhancement of worship.[46] Some churches see media as a marketing tool, others as simply a better way to communicate. Only occasionally have church leaders seen the potential for media to serve artistic purposes. At the 2005 Worship Technology Conference, advocates of "Experiential Video" for worship promoted the use of media for environmental art: "Discover how churches are moving beyond traditional use of video for lyrics, clips, and sermon support and into systems that create an atmosphere for worship and support the experience."[47] Few reading the conference's promotional brochure would realize that the origins of this "traditional use" actually went back more than a century.

Three worship models that have developed since the 1960s—the praise and worship service, the seeker service, and what some have called blended worship (traditional liturgy with elements borrowed from other kinds of contemporary services)—are now widely followed in United States churches. The first two models depend heavily upon multimedia support and projected graphics. Blended worship, too, can involve media when church leaders adopt the projection practices of the praise and worship and seeker service models. As baby boomers have become leaders in churches, many members of this first TV generation have found media in worship to be a natural evolution, even for worship with a denominationally defined worship order. When these baby boomers see contemporary worship in neighboring churches attracting and retaining young people, including their own children, they often conclude that worship needs today's media technologies and art.

Ironically, what qualifies as media art in most churches is on the level of the media art produced by secular artists in the 1970s and 1980s. Most churches lag at least twenty years or more behind the art world in the kind of media art they create or purchase and in how they imagine that media might be integrated within worship. Young people know it. On the fringes of churches in Australia, Canada, Germany, New Zealand, the United Kingdom, and the United States, some young Christian leaders who have grown up taking media for granted are moving toward closing that artistic gap.[48] They design worship services using an eclectic combination of symbols and practices from the Christian tradition along with multimedia more commonly found in dance clubs or parties. They create their own media art, not boxed in by any form of programmed church media art. With powerful laptop computers, they wield their media arts skills with an artistic freedom unknown to media producers in most large churches.[49] These young people, comfortable with creating their own video art, stretch their imaginations in the worship art they create and in how they incorporate it into their worship services. Typically, media is an integral worship element, rather than a supporting element. Not of interest to its creators is the tried-and-true presentation technology media art seen in churches since the late 1970s. These young people appear to be rediscovering the wonder of "illuminated walls" and of creating entire environments for meditation and stimulation, rather than for education or clarification. They seek experience of the Holy and encounter with each other in environments professional media artists would admire. They call the kind of worship they do "alternative worship."[50] In the experimentation of these young people, the vision of liturgical media art once created by the community at Liturgy in Santa Fe seems to have returned.

Notes

1. Michael Teres, "Projection," in *The Focal Encyclopedia of Photography,* ed., Leslie Stroebel and Richard Zakia, 3rd ed. (Boston, MA: Focal Press, 1993), 658.

2. Ibid., 658–59.

3. Michael Rush, *New Media in Late 20th-Century Art* (London: Thames and Hudson, 1999), 8–9.

4. Terry Lindvall, *The Silents of God: Selected Issues and Documents in Silent American Film and Religion 1908–1925* (Landham, MD: Scarecrow Press, 2001), 7.

5. Ibid., 6. Lindvall traces media history in this period by focusing exclusively on Protestant examples. He notes that Jews and Catholics also used these media in their efforts to reach out to congregants.

6. George J. Anderson, "The Case for Motion Pictures, Part II," *Congregationalist and Christian World* 95, no. 29 (1910): 78, in Lindvall, 47. A magic lantern was an early projector of color images painted on glass. A stereopticon was a combination of two projectors projecting two slightly different views of the same scene. When the two views were superimposed and projected one upon the other, viewers perceived the two-dimensional slides as a three-dimensional image.

7. K.S. Hover, "Motography as an Arm of the Church," *Motography* 5, no. 5 (1911): 84–86, in Lindvall, 52–53.

8. E. Boudinot Stockton, "The Picture in the Pulpit," *Moving Picture World* 14, no. 4 (1912): 336, in Lindvall, 79–80.

9. Ibid., 80.

10. Ibid.

11. Anonymous, "Moving Pictures as an Aid to the Church," *Current Opinion* 68 (1920): 226–27, in Lindvall, 229.

12. Ibid., 230; Anonymous, "The Motion Picture as a 'Handmaid of Religion,'" *The Literary Digest* 64 (1920): 46–47, in Lindvall, 235.

13. Ibid., 236.

14. Ibid., 238.

15. Ibid., 249–308.

16. Ibid., 251.

17. Ibid., 252.

18. Charles Johnson Post, "Motion Picture Madness," *The Christian Herald* 45, no. 26 (1922): 465–66, in Lindvall, 262.

19. Ibid., 269.

20. Ibid., 310.

21. Ibid., 311–12.

22. Kathleen C. Francis, "Amateur Photography," *Focal Encyclopedia of Photography*, ed., Leslie Stroebel and Richard Zakia, 3rd ed. (Boston, MA: Focal Press, 1993), 25.

23. Richard Couture (All-Pro Sound President and owner, Pensacola, FL), phone interview by author, February 2002.

24. Gabe Huck (liturgist and publisher, Chicago, IL), interview by author, February 2002, New York City; idem, e-mail correspondence with author, February 2002.

25. Couture interview.

26. See Redman, "The Praise and Worship Movement," *The Great Worship Awakening*, 22–46.

27. While the slides used for meditation often came from private collections, some came from published collections, such as the series by Gabe Huck, *Visual & Verbal Meditations* (Kansas City, MO: New Life Films, 1973).

28. "Mainline denominations peaked in their attendance in the 1950s, and then began an alarming rate of decline in the 1960s and 1970s." Douglas C. Mohrmann, "Megachurch, Virtual Church," in *Religion as Entertainment* (New York: Peter Lang, 2002): 31. For examples of how churches responded to this decline see James White, *New Forms of Worship* (Nashville, TN: Abingdon Press, 1971).

29. George Conklin (Pacific School of Religion retired professor of communications and media from 1973 to 1985, Berkeley, CA), e-mail correspondence with author, February 2002.

30. A major resource for the information on Liturgy in Santa Fe was a liturgical artist, Andrea (Drew) Bacigalupa, who helped to develop the chapel's slide approach, created slides, and orchestrated slides dissolved to music for meditation. See Andrea (Drew) Bacigalupa, "Liturgy in Santa Fe: 'Anything Less Won't Do,'" *National Catholic Reporter*, March 14, 1975; idem, "Santa Fe's Illuminated Walls," *Liturgical Arts* 39, no. 4 (1971): 101–3; idem, phone interview by author, February 2002. See also Clifford Stevens, "A Liturgical Pioneer," *The Priest* (1973): 24–27.

31. *Environment and Art in Catholic Worship*, 104–106, Bishops' Committee on the Liturgy, National Conference of Catholic Bishops, 1978, in *The Liturgy Documents: A Parish Resource*, 3rd ed., ed. Elizabeth Hoffman (Chicago, IL: Liturgy Training Publications, 1991), 337–38.

32. Willow Creek Church's leaders applied the recommendations of church growth movement evangelists who took a marketing approach to evangelization, an approach that had evolved from the 1950s teachings of a missionary who translated his international evangelization experience to domestic evangelization purposes. The church growth movement began in 1955 with the publication of *The Bridges of God* by missionary Donald McGavran. From his position as chair of church growth at the School of World Missions at Fuller

Theological Seminary in Pasadena, CA, McGavran influenced a generation of evangelical ministers who, in turn, have influenced many other evangelical and mainstream Protestant ministers. The megachurch phenomenon, based on a marketing model, has been one of the success stories of the church growth movement. See Erling Jorstad, "Church Growth Movement," *Popular Religion in America: The Evangelical Voice* (Westport, CT: Greenwood Press, 1993), 192–94.

33. Mohrmann, 32.

34. Ibid., 33.

35. Rush, 36.

36. Ibid., 38.

37. Michael Rush, "No Longer an Orphan, Video Art Gives Itself a Party," *New York Times,* 10 February 2002.

38. Examples of churches where liturgies incorporated media in the late 1970s, according to one article, included the Georgetown University campus church in Washington, DC, Calvary Presbyterian Church in Riverside, CA, an unnamed United Methodist church in Philadelphia, PA, St. Francis de Sales Cathedral in Oakland, CA, and an unnamed church in Lubbock, TX. Anne Michelle Ramagos, "Media in Liturgy: Why Not?" *Modern Liturgy* 5, no. 8 (1978): 6–7.

39. Mel White, "Using Electronic Media in Worship," *Leadership: A Practical Journal for Church Leaders* (1983): 96–97.

40. In 2002, Couture estimated that a "750-seater church" could get "a good media projection system for about $7,500 with $3,500 for the projector, about $1,000 for the screen, about $1,500 for a computer, and about $600 for the network software, and installation." Couture interview.

41. By the late 1990s, the video projector comparable in brightness (1,300 lumens) to the $100,000, 160-pound projector vendors would have installed in the mid-1980s might cost around $3,000 and weigh five to eight pounds. In 2002, the vendor providing that comparative data estimated, "Today, $100,000 will buy the brightest projection system (12,000 lumens) and weigh in the mid-200 pounds." Wayne Wagner, (Wagner Media owner, Houston, TX), phone interview by author, February 2002.

42. Christian Copyright Licensing, Inc. (CCLI), for example, provides this service internationally, http://www.ccli.com.

43. Wagner interview.

44. Robert Redman Jr., "Welcome to the Worship Awakening," *Theology Today* 58, no. 3 (2001): 370.

45. Ibid., 372.

46. Ken Holsinger, a Fowler Productions PowerPoint presentation for seminars on "The ABCs of Multimedia in Worship" (2002), received from

Thad Stalcup, (Fowler customer relations, Norman, OK), e-mail correspondence with author, February 2002.

47. Promotional brochure for 2005 Worship Technology Conference. See also Cathy Hutchinson, "Experiential Video: Churches are Moving from Static Information Transfer to Creating Visual Experiences," *Technologies for Worship Magazine* 11, no. 2 (2005): 48–50, 52, 54.

48. Andrew Jones, "Is this the Next New Worship?" *FaithWorks* 4, no. 4 (2001): 16–19, and "From Rock to Rave: The Emerging Face of Postmodern Worship" *Worship Leader* 10, no. 6 (2001): 20–22, 24, 26.

49. Since the mid-1990s professional video artists have contributed to the monthly Techno-Cosmic Mass in Oakland, California, a service inspired by British rave services that featured banks of video monitors. Kelly Durkin, (Sandboa Media video artist, Point Reyes, CA), phone interview by author, January 2003. For additional examples of the contributions of video and other artists to new forms of worship, see Eddie Gibbs and Ryan K. Bolder, *Emerging Churches: Creating Christian Community in Postmodern Cultures* (Grand Rapids, MI: Baker Academic, 2005).

50. Photographic examples of their efforts from services in England, Germany, New Zealand, and Northern Ireland are featured on their Web site, http://www.alternativeworship.org.

3 Media in Worship: Perils and Positive Possibilities

The use of media in Christian worship poses diverse challenges. The very effort of incorporating media into worship is a liturgical, technical, and aesthetic challenge for all involved. Furthermore, what worshipers experience through media on any given Sunday may challenge them in ways spiritual, moral, financial, and ethical. The focus of this particular chapter, though, is the challenges coming from a different group: critics who question whether media in worship is ever appropriate. The truth is that the use of media in worship has both perils and positive possibilities.

Perils

Critics' concerns about media in worship generally cluster around four issues: the degree of worshipers' *participation*—internal and external—in a service, the possibility of worship becoming *entertainment*, the potential for contamination from inclusion of *popular mass media*, and the temptation to *idolatry*.

Worshipers' Degree of Participation

Critics claim that the introduction of media in worship results in a decrease in worshipers' active participation and a consequent increase in worshipers' passive spectatorship. For worship traditions that typically expect members of the assembly to sing, to respond vocally, to reach out to others, to perform ritual gestures, or to move in ritual ways, increased worship time spent in spectatorship is problematic. In churches committed to liturgical reform and renewal, assembly members ideally know themselves to be the performers of worship, not an audience observing worship. As ritual performers, members of the assembly need to commit themselves in body, mind, and spirit. Research from multiple disciplines indicates that the less people's bodies are kinesthetically engaged, the less worshipers are "present" in the way liturgical reformers have envisioned.[1] "As pastors and worship leaders," explains evangelical worship consultant Sally Morgenthaler, "our job is to enable [relationship with God], to make participants out of spectators. We have to help people pour out what God pours in. Spectator worship has always been and will always be an oxymoron."[2]

Worship can be understood as the "rehearsal of 'right attitudes,'" according to philosopher Susanne K. Langer.[3] If participation in worship is intended as a model for how Christians are to go forth, to proclaim the gospel, and to be active in the world, they need to be full and active participants in worship, not simply passive observers. The more worshipers put their voices and the rest of their bodies into action, the more enriched will be their rehearsal for Christian living. The rehearsal of right attitudes is not a passive spectator sport.

Does media in worship cause worshipers to be spectators? Yes. When people are viewing and listening to media, they are spectators, just as they are when they are listening to a preacher, a choral work, or a soloist. These ritual moments usually require people to be somewhat still (depending on one's culture, of course) and, ideally, to attend to whatever communication or experience is being offered in whatever art form. In truth, to one degree or another, spectatorship is part of every church service. Even without media being included, some approaches to worship traditionally have called upon those present to do little more than sit, listen, and watch others perform the service. Any issues regarding worshipers' degree of participation must be addressed in relationship to the kind of service under consideration and the whole of the service.

When media and media art are included in worship, only the spectator can really say the degree to which she or he is actively engaged in a ritual moment. Contemplation, a very active internal form of participation, has a time-honored role in Christian tradition. Although usually identified more with private prayer, contemplation can have a place in corporate worship, especially during ritual silence or meditative music. Media in worship can likewise be a focus for ritual contemplation.

The fear (that media in worship renders everyone present more passive than they would normally be) seems based on underlying simplistic judgments of worshipers' capacity for reflection and for their active reception of media. Methodist professor of church and society Tex Sample says that spectacles—and by extension, spectators—have gotten an unjustified "bad rap."[4] Deeper reflection is in order.

To address seriously the issue of participation in worship that includes media, assumptions about worship participation and spectatorship need closer, critical examination. Regarding this worship topic, perspectives not normally taken into consideration come from ritual, media, and communications scholars.

Ritual studies scholar Ronald L. Grimes calls worship a "multimedium": "Ritual, like television *is* a medium of communication, an enacted one . . . a synthesis of drama, storytelling, dance, and art."[5] Another scholar of rituals, M. E. Combs-Schilling, defines ritual as "a circumscribed, out of the ordinary, multimedia event."[6] If worship is multimedia and a media event, then the work of media theorists who have investigated various aspects of spectatorship can be instructive.

To begin, media theory invites a critical examination of the assumption that media in worship necessarily diminishes people's role as participants. Ritual communications and media theorist Eric W. Rothenbuhler points out that, in ritual, spectators do participate as viewers and that "spectatorship is no simple social category; it is associated with a great variety of forms of participation in what can be a deeply meaningful experience."[7] People at sporting events know that spectating can be a very active participatory experience, though different from the kind of participation of the players on the field. People who watch plays, movies, and television programs can be drawn deeply into a drama, comedy, or television-mediated ceremony such as the wedding or funeral of a national figure.[8] Spectator participation can potentially affect people's attitudes and even trigger action. Think of those who watch news bulletins of catastrophes and immediately find some way to respond, whether through a monetary donation or through physically pitching in to help others recover.

During the last decades of the twentieth century, media theorists focusing on people's reception of media have concluded that people are more internally (and occasionally externally) active than some media and church critics would suspect. In general, these theorists find that media viewers are a "creative audience."[9] This research suggests that worshipers who view video footage in a service are most likely interpreting what media they hear and see projected. "People don't simply 'consume' media; they experience media images, symbols and messages as part of an ongoing flow of experience in their lives," communications scholar Stewart Hoover explains.[10] This longtime media researcher would appreciate liturgical theologian Dwight W. Vogel's related insight: "Participation in the liturgy involves us in a hermeneutical circle, whether we are aware of it or not, or name it that or not. After engaging in the liturgy, we may talk with one another about it. We may read about it. We may remember something about it."[11] Writes communications scholar James Lull, "Meaning is never self-evident. Meaning construction is processual and highly subjective. Symbolic power, thus, is exercised by message senders and message interpreters and users in the relatively open field of signification."[12]

Media researchers offer many characteristics in profiling the "creative audience." One characteristic can be commonly observed after worship in the fellowship halls of churches that regularly use media in their services: Media experienced in common stimulates discourse. In other words, it gets people talking. While drinking their coffee after worship, people often comment about the media they have just experienced, just as they may speak about the music or sermon. They might connect it not only with the day's Scripture message or song but also with other media they may have seen or with something happening in their lives.[13] In a study of a Wisconsin Congregational-UCC church that had created a media-intensive worship service, members reported that media art used in worship helped them to make more connections between worship and their lives. Parents found that they and their children talked about the morning's sermon at their Sunday dinner table, this because of the media that was related to it.

Spectatorship of any kind within worship may also provide a safe entry point for the uncommitted to be with a community. Spectators might come to see for themselves what being Christian means or demands. Spectating might be a visitor's first step toward membership, or not. Rothenbuhler explains:

> . . . spectating is a mode of access. It has limits, so if one's participation goes no further than spectating, then the meaning of the ritual will probably be thin and its effectiveness small. But spectating can provide access to other modes of participating; it can recruit viewers to engagement of festival, ritual, and other social forms.[14]

Thus, in church discussions related to worshipers' degree of participation in services that incorporate media art, simplistic understandings of participation and spectatorship are inadequate and must be questioned. To make media the scapegoat for worshipers' lack of active participation is to ignore other ways in which church leaders may turn worship into a performance to be watched.

The perils of spectatorship must be considered in light of the type of church service at issue, the proportion of media in worship, the functions media play within an entire service, and the nature of spectatorship in the rest of the service. Just because a media clip has been used in a seeker event (that follows a presentation model) does not preclude the possibility of that same clip functioning to encourage worshipers' active participation in a Sunday Eucharist (that follows a participation model). However, different types of church services call for different kinds and levels of participation. Decisions regarding whether, when, and how to use media must be made in the context of the role spectatorship plays in the entire worship event. For example, the leaders of Willow Creek Church, a megachurch influential in promoting seeker services, "try to be painstakingly clear that a seeker event is not worship."[15] Morgenthaler draws a sharp distinction between what she calls "seeker events" and "worship."[16] Obviously, in a seeker event, attendees are most likely spectators whose participation is relatively limited. The production level and values of such services tends toward that of spectacles. The opportunity for visitors at seeker events to be anonymous spectators is typically part of the churches' evangelization strategy.[17]

A significant problem arises, however, when other churches model their worship after seeker events without assessing critically the differences between seeker events and worship. Inadvertently, leaders may design their worship in ways that increase worshipers' sense of themselves as spectators and that decrease their sense of responsibility for their involvement in ritual action. By the way churches use media they may, in fact, give people present the impression that their *only* role is that of spectator. On the other hand, when churches use media to encourage people to sing, to respond, and to act in other ritual ways, they reinforce the opposite message, that is, that liturgy is the work of all present. The degree to which worshipers' bodies are engaged does matter. From active listening and active contemplation, to active bodily movement that literally gets people on the move, congregants' attentiveness and ritual actions can potentially affect the degree to which they might commit themselves to living out the gospel.[18]

Worship Becoming Entertainment

To some critics, media in worship is inappropriate because the presence of media contributes to worship becoming "merely entertainment."[19] Underlying this challenge are multiple presuppositions. Some church leaders see popular entertainment as being morally suspect and of questionable value in people's lives. Some Christians go so far as to condemn secular popular culture, including media, as being aligned with the "realm of evil."[20] Still others make the case that, specifically in worship, people should be engaged in more intellectually and spiritually elevated activities. Those voicing such opinions might agree with media commentator Neil Postman's accusation that today's media are the cause of people's "amusing [themselves] to death."[21] Accepting Postman's condemnation of media, Protestant theologian Marva Dawn suggests that entertainment in worship is contributing to the "dumbing down" of twenty-first-century worship.[22] The presence of media and media screens in worship potentially reinforces worshipers' expectation that services should be a form of spiritual entertainment, an "entertainment fix."[23]

Those critics who worry about worship becoming entertainment fear that the gospel, when packaged in entertainment genres, becomes diluted and that worship does not express the real substance of Christian faith.[24] One critic of contemporary worship, A. Daniel Frankforter, concludes, "When a church's standard for success is an ever-expanding congregation, it is hard for it to avoid deceptively packaging the gospel it sells." They end up offering "stones for bread."[25]

Also related to the general issue of entertainment in worship is the practice of churches that often incorporate media materials appropriated from popular mass media. Some critics argue that media technology and popular media are irredeemably tainted by manipulative capitalist agendas, commercialization, and commodification. They cannot possibly serve God.

Fundamentally at issue in debates about entertainment in worship is often the very acceptability of entertainment in *life*, never mind in worship. Christians have held divergent views. In some Reformed traditions where members may have been trained to see the movies, theater, and dancing as likely occasions of sin, "entertainment" of any kind can be suspect.[26] If, then, adding media technologies and art to worship were simply equated with "entertainment," media in worship would undoubtedly be unacceptable. On the other hand, some truly Catholic theologies recognize the potential for the things of the world—including entertainment—to become occasions for grace to erupt in ordinary people's lives.[27] This is not to suggest that Catholics alone recognize the things of the world to be potential occasions for grace. Anglican theologian William Temple describes humans as living in a "sacramental universe."[28] "The region of grace," writes Lutheran pastoral theologian Joseph Sittler, "is all that is, has been, and will be."[29] As Catholic sociologist-novelist Andrew Greeley puts it, "If grace is everywhere, it seems very likely . . . that it may be where people are."[30] People in the United States and elsewhere are engaged in popular media daily. As the bishops assembled at the Second Vatican Council proclaimed, "God, who creates and conserves all things by his Word, provides constant evidence of himself in created realities."[31]

When people equate media exclusively with the entertainment world, they may bring to their evaluation of media in worship not only their views on entertainment but also their disgust at the morals of some members of the entertainment industry. All media thus becomes painted with the same broad brush of condemnation (as was the earlier-mentioned case of churches rejecting the film industry in the mid-1920s).

Anglican theologian Michael Rusk tries to rescue the concept of "entertainment" as a valid element in church services. He makes the case that the powerful rhetorical skill of American Calvinist preacher

Jonathan Edwards can be considered "entertainment" of a holy kind. This eighteenth-century preacher employed vivid imagery of hell and of heaven in his revivals. In the sense that Edwards' sermons attracted people's interest and held their attention long enough for the Holy Spirit to activate listeners' religious affections and imaginations, this preacher used entertainment for the glory of God.[32] Walt Kallestad, pastor of a Lutheran megachurch and author of *Entertainment Evangelism*, notes: "Ever since I was a part of the gospel team movement in college I have seen how entertaining music and worship are not antithetical to effective worship. New forms can often enhance worship."[33] New forms of media can enhance worship, too.

Anthropologist Victor Turner points out that "entertainment," etymologically speaking, originated from words that relate to the creation of a "betwixt and between" experience. In this liminal space, he suggests, entertainment offers the kind of psychic, intellectual, and spiritual space that can potentially allow people's imaginations to entertain new insights.[34] In worship, then, certain kinds of entertainment can have their place, not only in attracting and evangelizing the uncommitted but also in moving worshipers to new understanding of Christ's call.

The Christian Reformed Church (CRC) provides its members with guidelines for discernment regarding a variety of arts in worship and directly addresses the complicated issue of entertainment in worship:

> The problem with the word *entertainment* is that five different people who use it mean five different things by it. Some would call *entertainment* whatever aims at people's feelings. That's too simplistic, since all worship should touch us at the feeling level. . . . Having said that, we also agree that entertainment does refer to tendencies in worship today that we would regard as troubling.[35]

Based on CRC guidelines, when would media in worship become entertainment? When media's use in worship is designed to generate a feeling response "to the exclusion of other important responses (for example, the response of the intellect and the will)," the CRC suggests, media falls into the category of entertainment, as it does when video magnification of a preacher leads to "a celebrity-like aura around a church's senior pastor."[36] In short, the use of media can be suspect when media draws disproportionate attention to the worshipers, the performers, or the art, rather than to the Holy One who is the Creator and to God's creation-in-need.

Contamination from the Inclusion of Popular Mass Media

As noted above, some critics question whether materials appropriated from popular mass media should be incorporated into worship. Communications scholar James Lull addresses the assumed hidden persuasions of the products of capitalist imperialism: "any argument that ideology and technology smother the senses with some corporate master plan—an idea basic to the media and cultural imperialism argument—does not stand up to the evidence. . . . in the final analysis no totalizing, controlling hegemonic effect is possible."[37] Other critics argue that the presence of popular mass media in a church service pollutes worship. Underlying this third perceived peril may well be biases against popular media and class-based prejudices.

Value judgments about what kinds of art are appropriate in worship can arise from value judgments about art in general. Calvin College professor of communications and arts William D. Romanowski explains that distinctions between what is considered "high art" and "low art" follow from elitist assumptions about culture and about who is considered cultured.[38] Fuller Seminary professor of theology and culture William Dyrness acknowledges that "for better or worse, the dominant artistic influences in the culture today are to be found among the popular arts, not among what used to be called high art."[39]

Popular media are popular because they satisfy what Gregor Goethals calls the "sacramental impulse—*the need to encounter invisible faith through visible forms.*"[40] Ordinary people need symbols that connect them with what is meaningful in their daily lives. "Popular culture . . . can provide important entry points for the gospel," Dyrness observes. "Those who would criticize use of popular culture as an entry point for the gospel should keep in mind that evangelism is calling out to people in urgent need: when you warn someone about an advancing avalanche you don't worry about your grammar."[41] Since some Christian symbols seem to have lost their power to speak to the imaginations of some people in media cultures, including perhaps Christians already present in the worship assembly, the juxtaposition of traditional symbols with symbols found in popular media may revitalize traditional symbols and may help in the communication of the gospel.[42]

Popular media provide a common ground, a common language, a bridge across which worshipers can connect their daily lives with their liturgical lives. "God can still work through popular art to affect people's lives," Romanowski insists. "The task for Christians is to discover and employ the most effective roles and purposes for popular art in service of our neighbor."[43]

Temptation to Idolatry

Two different forms of idolatry may be at issue when the question of the appropriateness of media in worship arises. Challenges to visual art of any kind within a worship space has a long history in Reformed Protestantism, according to William Dyrness. He explains that Protestants tend to privilege the ear over the eye "as the means by which God can be accessed in worship and devotion." He points out the main reasons given for Protestant rejection of the visual arts in worship: "Any visual attempt to mediate the presence of God is at best a distraction from this encounter, or at worst a temptation to idolatry."[44]

Whereas Dyrness highlights Protestant suspicion of image idolatry in general, Calvin College media theorist Quentin Schultze expresses concerns about a different form of idolatry related to media itself.[45] Media *technology* may become an occasion for sin. In the course of approaching worship as a production, some church leaders become mesmerized by the technology, what it can do, and how they can use it to control every production element of a service. Their creative and technical media staffs can become overly fixated with the technical possibilities of media tools. They can program and time their services to the second, thanks to the latest computer technology and software. In such cases, rather than the Spirit influencing the pacing of a worship service, media production requirements can instead drive the service. Morgenthaler calls this worship situation, "clock-driven servitude to hyperscheduled formats."[46] Media technology can become an "electronic golden calf," as Gregor Goethals puts it.[47] Media ministers can become engrossed in exploring the potential of their "technological toys" and lose their proper focus: using media for the building up of the reign of God.[48]

Furthermore, in a market-oriented world, church leaders and media ministers can come to desire more and more technology, to have the best equipment available as part of their competitive edge in selling their worship. "And," adds Morgenthaler, "when worship becomes a pawn of marketing, it ceases to have much to do with the expression and experience of a living, intimate relationship with the true God."[49] To avoid the fostering of idolatry, media systems and media art should be employed not simply because of their technological sophistication or attention-getting production values but because of their potential revelatory value. For the Latin word "video" itself means, "I see."

The Positive Possibilities

As has already been suggested, the use of media in worship may offer worshipers new insights, deepen their engagement in worship, and help them make connections between their daily life and their worship life. Some churches have taken up the challenge of including media in their services to *enhance communication*, to provide greater *liturgical access* for people with disabilities, and to encourage members' development of *spiritual sensitivity* and of their *sacramental imagination*. Let us consider more closely these positive possibilities.

Communication Enhancement in a Media Culture

Speakers trying to communicate with a group, large or small, know from experience that well-designed and thoughtfully used audiovisuals can enhance their ability to get their message not just across but through to their audience. As early as 1898, this desire to communicate clearly and memorably motivated some church leaders to use the audiovisual media of the day in worship and evangelism.[50] Especially in Protestant churches where the expectation of both minister and congregation is that preaching is teaching, church leaders have incorporated media to increase their members' ability to hear and retain the preacher's message. "After all, we're teaching them the most important lessons in their lives, so we need to teach for retention," explains Anthony D. Coppedge. "People remember about 30% of what they hear and about 70% of what they see in the same 24 hour period."[51] Communicating the message and getting it to stick is of prime importance.

Speakers trying to communicate with a group also know that they need to take into consideration the culture or cultures represented by those people gathered before them. They need to speak in the vernacular, whether that means using the culture's common spoken, printed or visual languages, or employing the culture's music, dance, or other arts. Communicating the message appropriately in the local context, using the local vernacular, is essential.

The case for the vernacular underlies the argument many advocates of media in worship have made for media's inclusion. This is not the first time such a case has been presented, of course. Throughout the history of Christian worship, as liturgical scholar Anscar Chupungco has repeatedly demonstrated, the liturgies and liturgical customs of diverse communities have incorporated elements of their culture's "vernacular."[52] Local language, rhetorical patterns for prayers, ritual body language, architectural spaces, times for feasts, ritual garb, and liturgical arts are among the many cultural elements that have been "baptized" for Christian liturgy. Over the centuries reformers and missionaries—whether Ulrich Zwingli in Switzerland, Thomas Cranmer in England, or Matteo Ricci in China—have stressed the importance of the gospel being shared and worship being celebrated in ways understandable to the local people. After the Second Vatican Council, most Catholic local churches quickly embraced the opportunity to worship in their own culture's vernacular language, rather than in Latin. In order to draw worshipers into greater participation in post-Vatican II worship in the United States, some composers turned to a musical vernacular, folk music, to encourage Catholics to sing. Post-conciliar Catholic worship has over the last four decades incorporated cultural elements as diverse as African and South Pacific textiles, visual arts, and dance;[53] Native American drumming; Filipino folk melodies; Hindu-inspired Indian ritual dance, flowers, and incense; and Mexican mariachi, jazz, and rock bands.

Chuck Smith Jr., son of the founder of the Jesus Movement of the 1960s that resulted in the nationwide network of Calvary Chapels, reminds other pastors, "A church that wants to provide worship in the *lingua franca* of mainstream culture, that is concerned with how intelligible it is to its host culture, will be interested in the current style, trends, and music of that culture."[54] Tex Sample insists that worship in what he calls today's electronic culture must be "Incarnational," because "our flesh is encoded culturally and historically and . . . we are socially constructed." Worship, he believes, must involve "indigenous engagement" with the culture.[55] Catholic liturgical scholar Mark R. Francis, agrees:

> The pastoral consideration of preparing the rites in light of the needs, religious dispositions and aptitude of the members of the assembly is the basis for what we today call the "inculturation" of the liturgy. Liturgical inculturation has as its aim seeing to it that the members of the assembly take their "full, conscious, and active part" in liturgical celebrations. Attentiveness to the culture (and cultures) of the members of the local church, then, is essential if worship is to communicate the good news of Jesus Christ in an effective way. At heart it is a matter of evangelization.[56]

In reaching out to people living in today's media cultures, pastoral leaders in local churches have come to realize that the "needs, religious dispositions and aptitudes" of their congregants and others whom they seek to draw through their church doors are different from those of previous generations. Regarding his own Reformed tradition, William Dyrness notes that, although "the Protestant imagination has been nourished uniquely by the spoken and written Word," an exclusively verbal diet is insufficient for today's worship services:

> Our children and their friends have been raised in a different world; they are often uninterested in our traditional word-centered media. Instead, they are looking for a new imaginative vision of life and reality, one they can see and feel, as well as understand. And their attention span for sermons and lectures is notoriously short![57]

The strongest advocates of media in worship, not surprisingly, are often the teachers who are members of a church. From their own training as educators, they know that worshipers of all ages possess multiple intelligences. Included among the seven intelligences identified by Harvard psychologist Howard Gardner are the ability to process language, whether oral or written, and the ability to deal with processing the visual and spatial world. Thomas Armstrong simplifies these two categories by referring to these intelligences as "word smart" and "picture smart." According to Gardner, people possess most forms of intelligences to some degree, but they typically have one that is their major way of processing reality.[58]

Much Protestant and Catholic worship today requires people to be "word smart," as any child in attendance would attest. Within any congregation in media cultures, though, an increasing percentage of those in attendance are likely to be more "picture smart." Comments Dyrness, "The contemporary generation has been raised and nourished by images; it has an inescapably visual imagination."[59] The introduction of media arts into worship potentially gives those who are "picture smart" a chance to enter more fully into the service.

For the "word smart" and the "picture smart" alike, certain kinds of media art—especially slide and video pieces created by church members themselves—not only enhance communication within worship but also encourage communication beyond it. As noted earlier, media in worship tends to stimulate dialogue after worship and beyond, say pastors and parishioners alike. For instance, after a Catholic Eucharist in which the homilist used footage of the United States civil rights movement and black civil rights leader Martin Luther King Jr., the pastor of an Oregon parish overheard teens asking their parents what they remembered of that time.[60]

Communication is basic to communal meaning-making. "Meanings are in people," notes Methodist minister and frequent communications commentator William F. Fore. Thus, all church leaders and media ministers need to remember with humility that "there are no meanings except as people give meanings to things and relationships."[61] Media alone cannot create meaning. It can, however, draw worshipers into a new or different degree of individual and communal meaning-making.

Greater Liturgical Access for People with Disabilities

Highly intellectual approaches to worship and preaching may not reach the hearts and minds of all those in attendance. If today's worshipers are to carry home the content of a service's message and to draw meaning for their lives, they may need points of entry into that material other than the cognitive. In advocating that Christian worship "come to its senses," Methodist liturgical theologian Don E. Saliers explains:

. . . the physical senses are crucial to the recovery of awe, delight, truthfulness, and hope. For worship depends upon our capabilities of sensing presence, of hearing, seeing, touching, moving, smelling and tasting. This is perhaps especially so when one or more of those senses is limited, as in specific disability, simply because Christian worship is physically, socially, and culturally embodied. . . And knowledge of God is never purely intellectual.[62]

Church services that are intentionally multisensory engage participants in ways different from services that depend heavily upon words that are spoken, written, read, recited, or sung.

For individual members of a congregation, the inclusion of media in worship can mean greater access to the worship experience itself. It can be a mark of hospitality. The leaders of a Church of the Brethren in Maryland intentionally have created what they call "a visually-driven worship experience" in an effort to make worship more accessible to their members who are deaf.[63] At a Catholic church in Oregon the pastor reports that those most enthusiastic about media art in their liturgies are the elderly who find the combination of audio and large visuals helpful in their participating more than previously.[64] A Lutheran church in Minnesota uses video magnification of baptisms and other liturgical action, especially for the sake of children who otherwise cannot see what is happening.[65]

Media in worship gives visuals to those who are linguistically challenged—the developmentally impaired or immigrants who do not yet speak the local language fluently—to help them understand what may be going on. In multi-lingual services, translations of Scripture or prayers can appear on media screens or other projection surfaces. For those worshipers who are visually impaired or blind, however, services heavily dependent upon visual reinforcement and video segments may put them at a disadvantage. Worship ideally includes a variety of communication arts, lest any worshiper be excluded from full participation.

Encouragement of Spiritual Sensitivity and Sacramental Imaginations

In the sixteenth century, Protestant reformer John Calvin wrote, "There is no spot in the universe wherein you cannot discern at least some sparks of glory."[66] In the twentieth century, Catholic theologian Karl Rahner insisted that an important task of Christianity was to stir the imaginations of believers so that they could discern those sparks and appreciate the presence of Absolute Mystery in their daily lives:

"The Christian of the future will be a mystic or he or she will not exist at all."[67] To become mystics ordinary Christians need to develop enhanced sensitivity to the mystery all around them. They need what Andrew Greeley has called "sacramental" imaginations, "to imagine God as present in the world and the world as revelatory instead of bleak."[68]

Catholic theologian Richard R. Gaillardetz suggests that the development of a sacramental worldview goes hand-in-hand with the enhancement of one's spiritual sensitivity to God in the everyday. For, he explains, "ordinary human activities and relationships are a privileged place for the encounter with God, [that] can help us cultivate the skills of discernment necessary to negotiate successfully the demands that this technological age places on us."[69] In churches where media—especially clips from the popular media of television and film—are consistently placed in an integral way within worship, worshipers can develop a habit of "looking for God" in their daily lives. When they experience appropriated popular media within a liturgical context, the worship context colors their interpretation of the media. They never see that media material in quite the same way when next they encounter it in their everyday lives. Instead, the media becomes associated in their imaginations with the Scripture, sermon, theme, or song with which it was connected in worship.

When media staff and church members create their own "homemade" video segments for worship, producing them either by using their own original footage and photography or by combining purchased or appropriated imagery and sound from other media sources, they engage in a creative discernment process that enhances their spiritual sensitivity and encourages their sacramental imaginations. Before they can produce anything, media staff must reflect on the function of this media piece within their worship and the make-up of their local congregation who will experience it. But, more importantly, they must dwell deeply upon the nature of the liturgical service itself: the day's Scripture, the service theme, and the liturgical season.

In the course of worshipers experiencing popular media and creating their own media art, they become engaged in a spiritual practice that, field research indicates, can bear much spiritual fruit. Worshipers may become more attuned to the divine in the world. They can also be stirred in powerful ways to attend to the needs of others whose suffering they may not otherwise have noted. Media and media art—in its creation and its reception—can become an occasion of grace. Of course, this is only a possibility. Just including media in a service does not mean any of these positive possibilities may occur. To tap into this potential, pastoral leadership and church laity benefit from regular, ongoing dialogue on the connections between liturgy and daily life, a matter we will explore further in chapter 5.

This chapter has outlined the major objections to and the cases for the use of media in worship.[70] While media has drawn the attention of critics at the local and national church level, media also has its proponents who have gladly taken up the challenge of integrating it into their church services. They are in the forefront of experiencing weekly what may result from letting media enter the church auditorium or sanctuary.

Perils do exist. Media can fall flat, confuse viewers, or be used manipulatively or unethically. For a variety of reasons, media can be inappropriate in local contexts. Within the overall church service itself, media can be out of balance or out of place. Media, used unreflectively, can focus the faithful gathered in ways that do not contribute to the communal work of liturgy and the worship of God. But this is also true for other liturgical arts.

The positive possibilities are already realities in some churches. Media can draw people more deeply into a worship service and encourage their participation. It can speak to them in ways other arts cannot. For the disadvantaged, media can provide increased opportunities to participate in worship. For many worshipers, media can become the catalyst that helps them make meaningful connections between their worship and daily lives. It can inspire them to take part in works of compassion and justice in the world. In short, current use of media in worship demonstrates that media technology and media art have the potential to contribute in a variety of ways to worshipers' encounter with God and each other. Media can even become liturgical art for a media culture.

This chapter has tackled issues related to media in worship from a theoretical perspective. The next chapter turns to matters practical. It presents critical frameworks that can guide local reflection upon media in worship. Using these frameworks, church people may avoid the perils and take advantage of the positive possibilities of media in worship.

Notes

1. "The 'body' has recently emerged as a major focus of analysis in a number of disciplines, reflecting the development and convergence of several lines of thought (e.g., ethnography, human and social sciences, neurobiology, gender studies, etc.). No longer the mere physical instrument of the mind, it appears that the image of the body is being reappropriated to denote a more complex and irreducible phenomenon, namely, the social person." Catherine Bell, "The Ritual Body and the Dynamics of Ritual Power," *Journal of Ritual Studies* 4, no. 2 (1990): 300.

2. Sally Morgenthaler, *Worship Evangelism: Inviting Unbelievers into the Presence of God* (Grand Rapids, MI: Zondervan Publishing, [1995] 1999), 49.

3. "A rite regularly performed is the constant reiteration of sentiments toward 'first and last things': it is not a free expression of emotions, but a disciplined rehearsal of 'right attitudes'." Susanne K. Langer, *Philosophy in a New Key: A Study in the Symbolism of Reason, Rite, and Art*, 3rd ed. (Cambridge, MA: Harvard University Press, 1974), 153.

4. Tex Sample, *The Spectacle of Worship in a Wired Word: Electronic Culture and the Gathered People of God* (Nashville, TN: Abingdon Press, 1998), 57–62.

5. Ronald L. Grimes, "Ritual and the Media," in *Practicing Religion in the Age of the Media: Explorations in Media, Religion and Culture*, ed. Stewart Hoover and Lynn Schofield Clark (New York: Columbia University Press, 2000), 228.

6. M.E. Combs-Schilling, cited in Grimes, ibid.

7. Eric W. Rothenbuhler, *Ritual Communication: From Everyday Conversation to Mediated Ceremony* (Thousand Oaks, CA; Sage Publications, 1998), 65.

8. An insightful examination of the degree to which people participate in live broadcasts of significant national or world ceremonies is that of Daniel Dayan and Elihu Katz, *Media Events: The Live Broadcasting of History* (Cambridge, MA: Harvard University Press, 1992).

9. Robert A. White, "Audience 'Interpretation' of Media: Emerging Perspectives," *Communication Research Trends* 14, no. 3 (1994): 1–32.

10. Stewart M. Hoover, "Religion, Media, and the Cultural Center of Gravity," in *Religion and Popular Culture: Studies on the Interaction of Worldviews*, ed. Daniel A. Stout and Judith M. Buddenbaum (Ames, IA: Iowa State University Press, 2001), 59.

11. Dwight W. Vogel, *Primary Sources of Liturgical Theology: A Reader* (Collegeville, MN: Liturgical Press, 2000), 8.

12. James Lull, *Media, Communication, Culture: A Global Approach*, 2nd ed. (New York: Columbia University Press, 2000), 162.

13. See Eileen Crowley-Horak, "Testing the Fruits: Aesthetics as Applied to Liturgical Media Art," (dissertation, Union Theological Seminary, 2002).

Available from Proquest Information and Learning. http:/proquest.com/ products_umi/dissertations/. ProQuest ID no. 726435071, publication no. AAT 3048887, ISBN 9780493632179.

14. Rothenbuhler, *Ritual Communication*, 219.

15. Morgenthaler, *Worship Evangelism*, 45.

16. Ibid., 44.

17. "A 'seeker-friendly' environment has as its cornerstone the freedom of observing from a distance without pressure to commit." Douglas C. Mohrmann, "Megachurch, Virtual Church," in *Religion as Entertainment*, ed. C. K. Robertson (New York: Peter Lang, 2002), 31.

18. Regarding the impact of ritual performance, Margaret Mary Kelleher notes "a common realization that individuals and communities embody meaning in their actions and that performance or praxis reveals and shapes personal and social identity." Margaret Mary Kelleher, "Hermeneutics in the Study of Liturgical Performance," *Worship* 67, no. 4 (1993): 301.

19. "The church cannot justify its existence by offering people the kind of momentary relief from pain and anxiety that entertainment provides—secular agencies do a much better job." A. Daniel Frankforter, *Stones for Bread: A Critique of Contemporary Worship* (Louisville, KY: Westminster John Knox Press, 2001), 162.

20. "Christians exhibit a wide range of attitudes about popular art, from sheer antagonism to complete acceptance. Some Christians identify unbelief with mainstream popular culture and practice varying degrees of abstinence. This *condemnation* approach can be seen in consumer tactics like boycotts, but it is perhaps more pervasive as an attitude that aligns Hollywood or popular culture with the realm of evil as opposed to the kingdom of God. If the popular arts are 'of the devil,' the only recourse for Christians is complete abstinence. For some churchgoers, then, avoiding 'secular' popular art altogether is the mark of a true believer." William D. Romanowski, *Eyes Wide Open: Looking for God in Popular Culture* (Grand Rapids, MI: Brazos Press, 2001), 12.

21. Neil Postman, *Amusing Ourselves to Death: Public Discourse in the Age of Show Business* (New York: Penguin Books, 1985).

22. Marva J. Dawn, *Reaching Out without Dumbing Down: A Theology of Worship for the Turn-of-the-Century Culture* (Grand Rapids, MI: William B. Eerdmans Publishing, 1995).

23. Morgenthaler, *Worship Evangelism*, 53.

24. "Within the church, some of the most technologically sophisticated worship services and the most elaborate musical productions can contain a lot of hype with little substance." Quentin J. Schultze, *Communication for Life: Christian Stewardship in Community and Media* (Grand Rapids, MI: Baker Academic, 2000), 84.

25. Frankforter, *Stones for Bread*, 48.

26. William D. Romanowski, *Pop Culture Wars: Religion & the Role of Entertainment in American Life* (Downers Grove, IL: InterVarsity Press, 1996), 36.

27. "The Catholic Imagination in all its many manifestations ([David] Tracy calls it 'analogical') tends to emphasize the metaphorical nature of creation. The objects, events, and persons of ordinary existence hint at the nature of God and indeed make God in some fashion present to us. God is sufficiently like creation that creation not only tells us something about God, but by doing so, also makes God present among us. Everything in creation . . . brings God among us." Andrew Greeley, *The Catholic Imagination* (Berkeley, CA: University of California Press, 2000), 7.

28. William Temple, *Nature, Man, and God* (London: Macmillan, 1940), 473.

29. Joseph Sittler, "Essays on Nature and Grace," in *Evocations of Grace*, ed. Steven Bouma-Prediger and Peter Bakken (Grand Rapids, MI: William B. Eerdmans Publishing, 2000), 153.

30. Andrew M. Greeley, *God in Popular Culture* (Chicago, IL: Thomas More Press, 1988), 93.

31. *Dei Verbum* (Dogmatic Constitution on Divine Revelation), no. 3, 18 November 1965, in *Vatican II: The Basic Sixteen Documents*, ed. Austin Flannery, rev. ed. (Northport, NY: Costello Publishing, 1996), 98.

32. Michael Rusk, "The Great Awakening: American Religion Comes of Age," in *Religion as Entertainment*, 7–26.

33. "Different styles attract different groups of people. In fact, some studies today suggest that more and more people are choosing a church more because of its style of worship than because of its theology or heritage. The style of worship, the language, the music, the preaching, the programs—all have at least as much influence on people's choice of a particular church as the substance has. While there is something to be feared in this shift, it is yet another change on which we do not have a vote." Walt Kallestad, *Entertainment Evangelism: Taking the Church Public* (Nashville, TN: Abingdon Press, 1996), 23.

34. Victor Turner, *From Ritual to Theatre: The Human Seriousness of Play* (New York: PAJ Publications, 1982), 121.

35. *Authentic Worship in a Changing Culture* (Grand Rapids, MI: CRC Publications, 1997), 81.

36. Ibid., 82.

37. Lull, *Media, Communication, Culture*, 223.

38. "[T]he commercial character of popular art can be used to judge it inferior to high art. The assumption is that popular art is 'not primarily produced in order to gratify the creative urge of its maker but primarily intended

to meet the requirements of a patron or a buying public,' as one scholar put it. But the arts always have a commercial base, and there are plenty of examples of artists having to appease a patron or market." Romanowski, *Eyes Wide Open*, 73.

39. William A. Dyrness, *Visual Faith: Art, Theology, and Worship in Dialogue* (Grand Rapids, MI: Baker Academic, 2001), 17.

40. Gregor Goethals, "TV Faith: Rituals of Secular Life," *The Christian Century* (1986): 414.

41. William Dyrness, "Can Americans still hear the good news?" *Christianity Today* (1997): 35.

42. "Filling this need [for meaningful public symbols] are the mass media, chiefly television, with its compelling, pervasive images. However shallow, they provide a web of meaning and values, and connect isolated groups, rendering visible our culture's invisible standards and goals." Goethals, "TV Faith," 414.

43. Romanowski, *Eyes Wide Open,* 71.

44. William Dyrness, "Experiencing God through the Visual: A Methodological Inquiry," (lecture, United Theological Seminary, September, 2002).

45. Quentin J. Schultze, *Communicating for Life: Christian Stewardship in Community and Media* (Grand Rapids, MI: Baker Academic, 2000), 118–20.

46. Morgenthaler, *Worship Evangelism,* 67.

47. Gregor T. Goethals, *The Electronic Golden Calf: Images, Religion, and the Making of Meaning* (Cambridge, MA: Cowley Publications, 1990).

48. "To attract people from our culture, some Christian churches depend upon glitz and spectacle and technological toys, rather than on the strong substantive declaration of the Word of God and its authoritative revelation for our lives. This tendency is blatantly demonstrated by an emphasis on 'Entertainment Evangelism,' without a correlative process for nurturing those attracted into deeper discipleship." Dawn, *Reaching Out without Dumbing Down,* 50.

49. Morgenthaler, *Worship Evangelism,* 18.

50. Terry Lindvall, *The Silents of God: Selected Issues and Documents in Silent American Film and Religion 1908–1925* (Landham, MD: Scarecrow Press, 2001), 1.

51. Anthony D. Coppedge, "Today's Visual Church," *Technologies for Worship Magazine* (July 1996), 41.

52. For many historical instances of the intersection of and exchange between liturgy and culture, see Anscar J. Chupungco, *Progress and Tradition* (Beltsville, MD: The Pastoral Press, 1995).

53. To view a variety of instances of liturgical inculturation, watch the video documentaries produced by Tom Kane, *The Dancing Church: Video Impressions of the Church in Africa* (New York/Mahwah, NJ: Paulist Press, 1991) and *The*

Dancing Church of the South Pacific: Liturgy and Culture in Polynesia and Melanesia (New York/Mahwah, NJ: Paulist Press, 1998).

54. Chuck Smith, Jr., *The End of the World . . . As We Know It* (Colorado Springs, CO: WaterBrook Press, 2001), 91.

55. Sample, *The Spectacle of Worship in a Wired Word*, 105–6.

56. Mark R. Francis, *Shape a Circle Ever Wider: Liturgical Inculturation in the United States* (Chicago, IL: Liturgy Training Publications, 2000), 8. Also see Anscar J. Chupungco, *Liturgical Inculturation: Sacramentals, Religiosity, and Catechesis* (Collegeville, MN: Liturgical Press, 1992).

57. Dyrness, *Visual Faith*, 21.

58. Thomas Armstrong, *Multiple Intelligences in the Classroom* (Alexandria, VA: ASCD, 1994), 39. Other intelligences he describes as logic, body, music, and people smart.

59. Dyrness, *Visual Faith*, 20.

60. See examples in "Liturgical Media Art" and case studies in "Voices of Experience," in Crowley-Horak, "Testing the Fruits," 82–200.

61. William F. Fore, *Mythmakers: Gospel, Culture and the Media* (New York: Friendship Press, 1990), 13.

62. Don E. Saliers, *Worship Come to Its Senses* (Nashville, TN: Abingdon Press, 1996), 14–15.

63. Church of the Brethren, Frederick, MD, for further information: http://www.fcob.net/deaf_fellowship/associate pastor for deaf ministries [14 March 2006].

64. Juniper Schneider, (St. Joseph Catholic Church pastor, Roseburg, OR), phone interview with author, August 2001.

65. Handt Hanson, (ELCA Prince of Peace Church, worship and music team leader, Burnsville, MN), e-mail correspondence with author, February 2002.

66. Cited in Dyrness, *Visual Faith*, 53.

67. Karl Rahner, "The Spirituality of the Church of the Future," in *Theological Investigations* vol. 20 (New York: Crossroad, 1981), 149.

68. Andrew M. Greeley, *The Catholic Myth: The Behavior and Beliefs of American Catholics* (New York: Macmillan Publishing, 1990), 4.

69. Richard R. Gaillardetz, *Transforming Our Days: Spirituality, Community and Liturgy in a Technological Culture* (New York: Crossroad Publishing, 2000), 45.

70. For a listing of eight other objections to television and video in the sanctuary and responses, see Michael Bausch, "Alternative Worship #6," *Church Worship* (1999): 5–6, 18.

4 Frameworks for Evaluation of Media in Worship

Opening an issue of *Technologies for Worship Magazine*, *Church Production Magazine*, or any other audiovisual trade publication designed to reach buyers in the "Houses of Worship" market, can be an eye-opening experience for the neophyte.[1] For ministers working in auditorium worship spaces, a writer provides tips on "Jazzing Up Your Stage" and becoming "one of the most well known churches in town."[2] Articles address technical issues such as how to analyze what kind of media system a church needs. The article, "Lights! Camera! Worship!" for example, "illustrates how lighting and visual media can be used to heighten the drama of a praise and worship program."[3]

Advertisers suggest that their products will help your church spread the message and build your congregation. Churches have grown from a small number of members to thousands, the magazines report, thanks in part to the media programming in their services. A vendor-produced magazine, *Vision*, intends "to help revolutionize the effectiveness of churches all across America and help them reach people for Christ in a way that they can relate to and understand."[4] Its premiere issue features a case study entitled, "From 36 to 1,900 in 18 months! How Journey Church is Reaching a City."[5] Via the magazine's website, readers can view and download some of this featured church's most popular slides and video clips.

Turn to the pages of evangelical- or Baptist-oriented worship publications, such as *Worship Leader* and *Faith Works*. There a reader finds advertisements that feature worship software containing pre-designed graphics for lyrics and Scripture as well as for pre-produced, theme-oriented graphic slides and video clips.[6] Church media producers looking for resources can also search the Internet for websites that provide graphic and video arts for worship.[7] One major Christian publisher offers a catalogue of software resources that contains more than one hundred CD-ROM and DVD collections of graphic and photographic backgrounds, nature-theme videos, animations, and other professionally produced media art for worship.[8]

For those new to this media-in-worship field, wading through all of these resources can be bewildering, if not overwhelming. Truth be told, church leaders and volunteers could easily lose focus on why they are seeking this material in the first place: worship. Local church leaders need a method for evaluating their use of media in worship, whether that media is commercially produced or home-grown. The method set forth here begins with worship, not media. Designed to be used by local worship leaders and worship team members, this analytical approach provides four frameworks for assessment and reflection: *overall worship context, functions of media in worship, liturgical and media aesthetics,* and issues of *ethics and justice.* Questions drive this process.

Framework I **Overall Local Worship Context**	1) functions and forms of local worship 2) liturgical actions in a particular form of worship 3) particulars of a faith community 4) worship space and overall environment
Framework II **Functions of Media in Worship**	1) to convey information 2) to encourage participation 3) to reinforce or enrich oral communication 4) to open up an interactive space—within and outside us—for discovery 5) to provide beauty

Framework III	1) liturgical aesthetics (appropriate, fitting, integral)
Aesthetics for Liturgical Media Art	2) media aesthetics (graphic, photographic, video arts, and performance arts)
	3) liturgical media aesthetics
Framework IV	1) responsible resource allocation
Issues of Ethics and Justice	2) living wages for technical and media staff
	3) licenses and copyright permission
	4) social justice issues
	5) diversity in people imaged and invited to contribute
	6) diversity in media art
	7) diversity in metaphors for God

Framework I: Analysis of Overall Local Worship Context

In analyzing media in their community's worship, church leaders need first to address four major areas related to their overall worship context: (1) the functions and forms of their worship, (2) the liturgical actions involved in a particular form of worship into which they want to incorporate media, (3) the particulars of their faith community, and (4) the spaces and overall environment in which their worship occurs. Only then should they turn to issues related to media.

One church's approach to the use of media may be entirely appropriate within its worship context. But if the leaders of a church down the street try that same approach, they may well find the media simply does not "fit." Why? Likely because they have not respected the functions and forms of their own worship before they imported the media model from the neighboring church. To avoid that mistake, church leaders advisedly should start their critical analysis with basic questions about their own worship: What are the functions of the communal service into which media might be incorporated? What is the form of worship that has resulted from the church trying to serve those worship functions? The answers to these starting questions about worship are foundational.

1. Functions and Forms

In examining any worship service, it is important to remember that form generally arises out of function, not vice versa. For instance, because the function of a Reformed service historically has been to prepare hearts and minds to hear the Word proclaimed and preached, the order of liturgical actions (the form of worship) within Reformed preaching-centered services has evolved to serve that ultimate function.

During the last decades of the twentieth century, churches with liturgical traditions and orders of worship began modifying their forms of worship because they wanted them to function differently. When they wanted to attract a different group of people, some churches turned the preaching service into something that would function more as a non-threatening lecture about spiritual and life issues. Other churches added elements of entertainment to attract and to keep people's attention. When churches wanted to engage people's emotions in a more affective experience of worship, some took musical elements of Pentecostal praise and worship services and added them to the opening of their service. Because of the mixing and matching of service elements that has been occurring, leaders responsible for serious reflection on their own worship may not be able to identify its function and form by what appears on the church bulletin or local newspaper ad. They may need to get back to basics: What kind of service is it? What is supposed to happen within this service? How does this community understand this service?

These questions about the overall functions and forms of a community's worship may seem simple to answer and even too basic to consider. But the very diversity of Christian worship today, a consequence of churches importing elements into their local worship from worship of other traditions, means that these questions must be asked. To rush into discussion of what media to use before really appreciating the function and form of the worship into which it might be incorporated puts the proverbial cart before the horse. Any media used needs to be integrally related to the worship, rather than an add-on.

For those churches celebrating the Christian liturgical year and offering a wide range of liturgical forms of daily and seasonal prayer, each ritual occasion demands careful analysis before media is introduced. Consider how different are the forms, functions, content, and actions of worship involved in the following events: evening, night, and morning prayer; Taizé- or Iona-style ecumenical prayer services; pilgrimages; Reformation Day; patronal saints' feast days; benediction and adoration of the Blessed Sacrament; All Soul's Day, All Saint's Day, and Day of the Dead services; Advent, Christmas, Epiphany, and Baptism of the Lord liturgies; Lenten services, including Ash Wednesday, Stations of the Cross, Tenebrae services, parish retreats and missions; Easter Triduum services, including those for Maundy or Holy Thursday, Good Friday, Holy Saturday, Easter Vigil, and Easter Sunday; the Easter season through to the celebration of Pentecost; and remembrance of Jewish and Islamic holy days or of other ecumenical occasions. One-size-fits-all media certainly does not apply in these very diverse worship forms, at these very diverse times, within a particular community's celebration of their liturgical year.

2. Liturgical Actions

Worship is an activity of embodied beings. Another aspect of analyzing the overall worship context and the appropriate use of media in a particular service is, therefore, to examine the kinds of liturgical actions that occur, the sequence in which they occur, and the purposes of those actions. Consider the great variety of ritual actions that might occur in a service. Some actions involve physical movement of some or all of the worshipers: welcoming, gathering, processing, standing, sitting, gesturing, bowing, kneeling, genuflecting, handshaking or embracing as a sign of welcome or peace, making signs of the cross, anointing with oil, carrying objects in a ritual way, presenting objects or people, lighting candles, reverently touching parts of a body in a blessing, kissing a cross or icon, baptizing, sprinkling with blessed water, or blessing members with hands raised. Some actions are verbally and musically performed: praising, thanking, lamenting, offering, petitioning, preaching, proclaiming, storytelling, singing, professing, confessing, accepting, affirming, testifying, witnessing, prophesying, and committing. Some ritual actions may be undertaken silently: meditating, remembering, adoring, pleading, praying, listening, and watching. For the service into which media might be integrated, what is the order of liturgical actions and who performs those actions, where and when? Only by understanding the liturgical actions called for in a particular form of worship can leaders ask: In what ways might the use of media help, hinder, or distract the baptized from performing any of these liturgical actions that are rightfully theirs?

3. Particulars of a Faith Community

Also affecting whether, when, and how media might be used are factors regarding the specific faith community engaged in that worship. Know thy assembly! What is the composition of the specific congregation for a given worship event? What percentage female and male? What age groups are represented? What economic and social levels? What percentage of those in attendance would be considered or consider themselves to be churched, unchurched, seekers, or visitors? What ethnic and racial mixture is present? What language groups? How would participants identify their sexual orientation? How many are married, single, divorced, or living with domestic partners? In any congregation, one-fifth to one-fourth of those present may live with various forms of physical, sensory, developmental, or emotional disabilities. How would media assist or add an obstacle to their participation? How many worshipers present might be economic or political immigrants or corporate transplants from other areas of the country or world? Knowing a congregation well is critical, not only to effective preaching and communication of any sort, but also to effective and sensitive use of media in worship.

Twenty-year-olds perceive media differently than baby boomers. To young adults, media is such an integral part of their lives that its use in worship is simply taken for granted. Consequently, the media within the experimental form of "alternative worship" that some young people create looks nothing like media projected in baby boomer-oriented megachurches. Abstract video art typically found at dance parties, or video designed to provide mood backgrounds, may be projected onto multiple surfaces within the worship space. Much graphic art may not convey content but, rather, suggest a mood or provide a kind of visual and auditory energy for a section of worship. Media is not limited to projection on a media screen or screens. Many surfaces display media. Images from church history might be visually mixed with abstract computer art and be evocative and poetic.

4. Worship Space and Overall Environment

Many of the issues that must be considered with respect to media decisions for particular worship spaces involve aesthetic questions, which are posed below in Framework III. As a preliminary matter, though, before introducing any media at all, local leaders must assess the physical space and the worship environment already present and the effect the presence of media might have on worshipers within it. Is the size of the projected media sufficiently large for media content to be easily seen? Can an appropriate number of projection locations be provided, given the configuration of the space and the number of worshipers? Will a TV monitor, screen, or projection equipment disrupt the existing harmony of the architecture, limit the flexibility of the space, or interfere with liturgical action? Does the existing space already have walls, ceilings, columns, or soffits that could serve as projection surfaces? Will stained glass windows, crosses, or works of art have to be covered to show media? Retrofitting Neo-Gothic or Romanesque-style churches that already have liturgical art present, or other churches that contain large windows that let in abundant sunlight, requires special consideration before media projection of any sort might be introduced. A thorough assessment of the existing space and environment is bound to reveal some limitations, even in storefronts and auditoriums where little or no competing religious art and architecture is present. Such an assessment might also lead to the discovery of creative opportunities for the introduction of media that had not been previously considered. Temporary projection surfaces may be a hanging white bed sheet, white foam-core board, or even a weather balloon. A large draped swath of fabric or light-colored textile might serve double duty as environmental or textile art and as media projection surfaces. Worship spaces in which projection may not work during the day might be more hospitable to media art during night services.

For instance, the pillars of St. Patrick's Catholic Cathedral in New York City can, at first, be thought of as an obstacle to the use of media in that space. But they also support small video monitors so that worshipers who are far from the altar area, or those whose vision is obstructed by the pillars themselves, may see the liturgical action. For the same reasons, plasma screens are attached to the pillars of St. Patrick's Catholic Cathedral of Armagh in Ireland. The Menlo Park Presbyterian Church in Silicon Valley, California uses two large sanctuary screens flanking their central stained glass window plus video monitors in side areas where members might not be able to see the central screen.[9] Should media be introduced into any worship space, it needs to be projected and displayed in a way that is respectful of the overall environment and does not visually or aurally compromise the space's primary purpose: to provide a physical environment conducive to the worship of God.

In sum, no introduction of media into worship should occur without at least some basic consideration of the overall worship context along all four dimensions noted in Framework I. This analysis is the first step in determining if, when, and where in a particular church or service media might serve as an integral element that offers a new dimension otherwise unavailable. Leaders might well determine that media should not be used at all, especially if other liturgical arts would contribute more or be more appropriate.

Framework II: Analysis of the Functions of Media in Worship

Framework I deals with worship: how it functions; what form it takes; who does the work of worship; and how, where, and when they do it. Framework II focuses on the media itself as one liturgical element within that overall worship context. Church leaders can use this framework to pose questions related to the current or potential use of media in a specific worship event: How does this media function? What is it that we hope this media will do within the service? In what way would this kind of media offer a dimension that would otherwise be unavailable?

Media in worship potentially functions in multiple ways and dimensions. Generally speaking, though, media in worship can function in five ways. The first three ways represent primarily communications functions: (1) to convey information, (2) to encourage participation, and

(3) to reinforce or enrich oral communications. Typically, media serving in these ways goes in one direction, toward the congregants, with the hope that worshipers will receive it. However, media in worship can also function as art, as an occasion for encounter, and may be experienced as epiphanic. It can (4) open up an interactive space—within and outside us—for discovery, and (5) provide beauty. Media intended to serve these artistic functions demands more of those who experience it, since less guidance is given on how one interprets the media. Media operating as art invites those who encounter it not only to be deeply engaged in its interpretation but also to be potentially challenged by inherent tensions and questions intentionally but unanswered.

Categorizing media functions in this way is a conceptual tool designed strictly for the purposes of evaluation. Making distinctions in how media functions can help church leaders begin to sort out how media might contribute to their worship. In practice, media as an element in worship may serve multiple and even simultaneous functions. In Framework II, the distinction being made between communications and artistic functions is merely a way to highlight important differences. Media in worship, since evangelical use of it in seeker services and Pentecostal use of it in praise and worship services, has been primarily for communications purposes—to aid in evangelization by communicating the message more effectively or to provide projected lyrics so that worshipers' hands are free to express themselves as the Spirit moves them. What has been little attended to is the potential for media in worship to function as art (see definition in chapter 1).

Communications are not necessarily art, although they may be when skillfully and artistically crafted. A broadcast news program communicates. Its producers are not trying to create art. A movie communicates, but its producers typically *are* striving to create art. All art is intended to be communicative, but not all communications are intended to be experienced as art.

Communications functions:

1) Convey information

During the last three decades, media's simplest and most common function in churches has been instrumental, that is, to convey information. Welcome messages, announcements, or indications of the theme or Scripture-of-the-day come in a variety of forms, such as simple text graphics, texts superimposed over images or other visual art, video clips, or some other combination of media.

2) Encourage participation

A common instrumental function of media in many churches is to encourage participation. The display of projected congregational refrains, hymn verses, or praise lyrics invites worshipers to look up and to sing out. Congregants may pray in unison thanks to prayers projected on a screen. In some churches, worshipers together read Scripture passages, either aloud or in silence. Worship leaders hope that by encouraging congregants to encounter the Scripture in the speaking, in the listening, and in the reading, these congregants may enter more deeply into reflection on the passage. Such multi-sensory practices may address worshipers' multiple intelligences. In these situations, media functions in ways comparable to a worship aid, hymnal, or prayer book. What is to be read, spoken, or sung is now simply being projected. However, pastoral musicians know that lyrics presented as text alone—either printed or projected—function differently from lyrics presented with a melodic line that people can potentially follow. Each presentation format has its advantages and disadvantages. Mindful of that reality, Prince of Peace Church in Burnsville, Minnesota, offers both lyrics projected and music printed in a worship aid. Its worship and music team leader explains that on the very first Sunday that his team projected lyrics, the volume of the congregation's singing doubled. In this Evangelical Lutheran Church in America (ELCA) setting, not to provide musical notation "is offensive to twenty percent of the congregation who are musicians and others who prefer to have the musical notation available." As a practical matter, the worship leader adds, if the media projection does not work, the congregation can still sing.[10]

Media used for a different liturgical purpose—to direct participants to take action other than singing—may include projected texts, graphic symbols, photographs, or animated or live action footage. A single word or graphic image may signal the time for people to come forward for communion, an altar call, or foot washing. A single projected image or some non-textual video footage, used in a way similar to an icon, invites participants' active contemplation and calls them to see through the images to the reality symbolized.

Each week for the emerging worship of Church of the Apostles, an ELCA-Episcopal "church plant" in Seattle, Washington, an artist who is a member of the community creates montage-style images overlaid with minimal text. These graphics announce each section of the service, provide ritual responses for participants, and direct worshipers to participate in various activities and ritual actions. This liturgical art is designed with skill and an aesthetic style attractive to those in their twenties and invites them into the actions of their worship.[11] At the ELCA Community Church of Joy in Glendale, Arizona, projected graphics also signal different portions of the service and suggest actions participants are expected to take. At the Episcopal Falls Church, Falls Church, Virginia, an evening service for Gen-X adults has used projected text to support participants' recitation of prayers from the Book of Common Prayer, prayers many of the twenty- and thirty year-old worshipers would otherwise not know by heart.[12]

3) Reinforce or enrich oral communication

In addition to conveying information and to encouraging participation, media may be used to reinforce and enrich oral communication in diverse ways. The difference between "information" and "communication" is significant. As professional communicators know, providing information is a matter of "giving out" content, whereas communications means "getting through," of actually reaching and connecting with a targeted audience so that they may come to know, think, do, feel, or believe something about what has been communicated. The appropriate communication of content is paramount. A preacher might employ a visual metaphor to reinforce a textual point, to help congregants know something about a proclaimed biblical passage, or to make accessible content that might otherwise be inaccessible to those who think more visually. By juxtaposing her words with a movie clip or video vignette, the minister might convey a sermon theme in a way that moves listeners to new insight. Video clips— both custom produced and edited from feature films—are commonly used at the McLean Bible Church, a megachurch in McLean, Virginia, and in many other churches whose leaders have decided to emulate successful strategies employed originally in seeker services.[13]

Video magnification (also known as image magnification or IMAG) is the live, simultaneous video recording, enlargement, and projection of liturgical actions, persons, or objects onto a large surface so that all may see and hear what is being presented. Video magnification serves to reinforce and enrich oral communication. People read lips more than most realize; they read body language, too. Being able to see a speaker's face and body more clearly may aid listeners' reception of the speaker's message. Video magnification can be done at various production levels. The most basic production level is simply to point the camera, shoot the action, transmit the video feed, and project whatever the single camera shoots. However, at a professional production level, this media production-and-transmission technique requires the technical and artistic skill of many media production team members and, as concert goers can attest, can itself produce a form of media art. For many reasons, though, church leaders should ask regarding video magnification, "Why use it at all? To what end?" Determining whether to use video magnification is a delicate issue. Only a local church can determine whether this media option, in their particular overall worship context, is a necessity and whether its use is in keeping with their community's understanding of worship of the One God to whom worship is due.

Clearly, the three functions of media in worship cited above are little different from the functions of media in educational, institutional, conference, work, or concert settings. They are primarily *communications* functions. Media may be employed and designed to function beyond their primary communications role, and sometimes media may actually also function as art.

Artistic Functions:

When the media in worship stands on its own and is designed in such a way as to invite viewers' active participation in its interpretation, media moves beyond being simply an element of presentation technology and becomes what may legitimately be called media art. It is intentionally designed to be evocative and communicative in multivalent ways, yet clear enough to require no explanatory comment. When a minister adds commentary before ("As you'll see in this video . . .") or after ("In other words . . .") a video vignette, it can flatten the potential impact and limit the freedom of viewers to engage in active interpretation. Even a single, powerful metaphoric photograph can "speak" in ways that, on its own, enriches whatever has been or will be said or sung. Such juxtaposition may result in a worshiper's grace-filled epiphany. At St. Joseph's Church in Roseburg, Oregon, a single photo of a local river with fog hovering above it has served as a projected media art "icon." Shown during the singing of Psalm 141:2, "Let my prayer rise before you as incense," the photo invites worshipers into a post-psalmody time of silent meditation.[14]

4) Open up an interactive space

An artistic function of media in worship is to open up an interactive space—within and outside us—for discovery. "Space" can be internal or external to the worshiper. Media art functioning metaphorically potentially opens up a contemplative *internal* space within a person who encounters it. It can trigger the imagination. It may allow a person to entertain an idea or emotion he or she might otherwise not have dared consider or feel. It may provoke a sense of wonder. It may surprise. It may even raise one's blood pressure or pulse! Because "art is symbolic in nature," it can manifest two of the six common characteristics of symbols described by Protestant theologian Paul Tillich: to "open up levels of that reality which would otherwise remain closed" and to unlock dimensions and elements of one's soul which correspond to the dimensions and elements of reality."[15] Media art may cause an insight that explodes inside a person to such an extent that the art makes room for discovery of The Other who is Holy Wisdom. It may also open a space for a worshiper to interact with "the other," another human being who is physically near but who might otherwise be ignored, perhaps a person who lives without a home or with mental illness. Encounters with such media art may open up a heart previously closed or hardened by life.

A member of Union-Congregational UCC Church in Waupun, Wisconsin, created a music video for one of their services based on the country song by Collin Raye, "What If Jesus Came Back Like That?" He juxtaposed haunting photographs of people who were homeless, babies hooked on crack, and people down and out, with the song's challenging lyrics. Upon viewing the music video, a woman in her thirties sat stunned. When asked what had happened, she responded that she finally understood her mother. For all the years of their growing up, she and her siblings had never understood their United Methodist mother's constant volunteer work with people who were hungry or poor. The children actually ridiculed their mother for her works of charity. The encounter with the music video, with its moving montage of song lyrics and photographs, opened a space in the daughter's heart that day: "I finally understand. My mother saw Jesus in them all."[16]

Media art may also create an interactive external physical space for discovery, through what has become known as installation art. In this kind of art, media is understood as only one among many art elements that may be employed in the creation of a space into which people enter and in which they interact, emotionally and even physically. Installation art invites people into active engagement with media, materials, and other people. Active participation is a key element of this art form that has its historical roots in early twentieth-century experiments and that became a more complex artistic endeavor in space and time in the mid-1960s: "Meaning is no longer given, residing in the object until discerned by the perceptive viewer, it is something that is made in the encounter."[17]

As one of "a small group of artists who were making works not as 'video artists,' but as artists who happened to use video,"[18] Bill Viola has since the mid-1970s created video installations that often are "deeply spiritual and contemplative works, capturing the essence of death, birth, and a variety of transcendent experiences of life."[19] His video installations have appeared mounted to the great western door of the Anglican Cathedral of Durham in northern England and nestled in a side altar area in the Episcopal Cathedral of St. John the Divine in New York City.

At Durham, video was shown of a naked man who rises from blue-black depths, "breaks the surface," "releases a long-held breath from the depths," and "sinks into the depths of the blue-black void once more, returning to his origin as a shimmering, moving point of light." Entitled *The Messenger*, the video repeats this sequence, thereby "describing the constant circulation of birth and death, and functions like a great cycle of respiration in the space," explains the artist.[20]

Water, again, plays a role in the three scenes that ran simultaneously, side by side, in the darkened side altar space in the New York cathedral. Projected on three screens was Viola's "Nantes Triptych" that slowly revealed three life stories. "Three large-scale panels of projected video images form a configuration based on the triptych altarpiece form," Viola explains. Images of his mother dying and of his wife giving birth flank a central panel, where "an image of a clothed man underwater is seen moving through alternate stages of turbulence and undulating stillness."[21]

In each case, Viola created a form of environmental art that potentially transformed the experience of worshipers who encountered it. His video and sound works literally changed the worship space itself and created a "space" of interaction within the hearts, minds, and imaginations of those worshipers who encountered his video frescos about life, death, and resurrection. "In the traditional manner of great art, Viola provokes the heart by leading the mind to avenues of contemplation and self-discovery. In so doing, the art provides the basis for an experience best described as transcendent—a curious word to use at the end of the age of mechanical reproduction, yet the only word that applies."[22]

In James Chapel at Union Theological Seminary in New York City, during a worship service designed to bring home the reality of AIDS around the world, congregants had the opportunity to walk to a space for contemplation and to interact with media at multiple locations. Laptop computers were placed on stands throughout the chapel. During a meditation period, the worship leaders invited the participants to walk over to the computers to read brief on-screen texts that offered testimonies from people living with AIDS or that provided statistics regarding the worldwide scope of the spread of HIV/AIDS. Each station featured texts from a specific continent. Participants had many choices for interaction with the stories provided by the media material, many opportunities for discovery. They could wander randomly from station to station or remain for a time at a single station. They could page through the texts on the laptop screens or simply stay at one computer and read many screen pages about the plight of the people living on one continent. At each station they could read aloud from those texts or offer a silent prayer. All worshipers present had the option to remain seated and to absorb the texts projected on large screen. They could also choose to close their eyes and not interact with any of the media, of course.[23] Individual choice regarding how and to what degree participants interact with the media is an important element of multi-stational art. Obviously, what each person may discover in the interaction will vary.

The point of such worship encounters is not for people to encounter technology. It is for them to be in intimate relationship with Absolute Mystery ever present and ever absent. It is to give them a chance to experience the liberation of entering a space, inside or outside of themselves, in which they can be open to God's loving self-communication, grace.

5) Provide beauty

The second artistic function of media in worship is to provide beauty. Beauty "is both the revelation of goodness and truth . . . and the revelation of the absence of goodness and truth."[24] In both cases, liturgical media art can open up a space into which worshipers can enter both spiritually, emotionally, and cognitively and discover something about God, God's creation, and each other.

Aesthetician Elaine Scarry argues that two forms of created beauty are distinguishable: "perpetuating of beauty that already exists; originating of beauty that does not yet exist."[25] Media that is art can serve in both capacities and need not be a high-tech video installation to do so. Photographs or simply edited video footage can display for contemplation the exquisite beauty of the world so that congregants may be moved to give due praise and thanksgiving to the Creator. Active contemplation of natural beauty in worship deepens one's worship of the One who is Beauty.

Community members can purchase or create their own media art that originates "beauty that does not yet exist" or that reveals beauty usually not noticed. Even when such works focus on subjects other than the wonders of nature, they may still lead to experiences in which worshipers sense the divine in the world. For example, a video presenting a community member engaged in works of mercy and justice may provide beauty—the beauty of a compassionate, committed heart. Similarly, a computer-generated animation of the structure of a molecule or colorful images of galaxies might, in the vibrant display of their complex patterns, provide beauty. Even constantly changing abstract pattern of light and color can be perceived as possessing beauty.

Here it must be emphasized that the five functions of liturgical media art presented above are not mutually exclusive. The final two functions, though, call for all media to be something more than "flat-minded literalism"[26] or didactic material, even when that media's primary purpose is communications. For example, in Liturgy in Santa Fe in the 1970s, local parish artists married the text of unison prayers with medieval-style illumination and calligraphy. When this work of calligraphic art was projected, it both encouraged participation in the recitation of prayer and provided beauty in the "media chapel." Media that is created for the purposes of conveying information, encouraging participation, and reinforcing and enriching oral communication is, ideally, media that has been artfully created. A well-designed Power-Point graphic, a single poignant photograph, projected lyrics, and a sermon illustration—when artfully created or appropriated, skillfully and sensitively integrated, and used appropriately within the overall liturgical actions of a service—can all provide beauty.[27]

What constitutes beauty will necessarily vary from place to place and culture to culture because beauty is relative to the aesthetic values and traditions of the community in which it is encountered. In order to appraise something as providing beauty in worship, one first needs to have eyes and ears trained to perceive it and some standards by which that appraisal may be made. In offering media art intended to provide beauty, the media artist knows and works within those standards to some degree, otherwise the art cannot communicate to members of the community. Media art in worship is communal art, ritual art. It comes under Nicholas Wolterstorff's definition of "tribal art" because it is intentionally created as something of and for the "tribe," not simply of and for the artist.[28] Thus, the community plays its own role as critical receivers of that art. The perception of something as art that provides beauty involves the interaction of the people who conceive and create it, what they have created, and the people who experience that creation. It is a dialogue, an encounter, an occasion for possible transcendence and transformation for those who create and for those who receive the creation. To discern beauty in media created for worship or for any other circumstance, "There is a discipline of seeing, just as there is anything we would do well."[29]

In worship spaces devoid of other forms of visual art, such as auditorium or gymnasium worship settings, the introduction of beauty through visual arts, including media arts, can be particularly important. Increasingly, Protestant liturgical scholars and worship conference speakers have urged church leaders in Calvinist Reformed and evangelical traditions to consider ways of using the arts beyond the typically predominant verbal and musical arts.[30] Scarry declares that "the absence of beauty is a profound form of deprivation."[31]

Within worship spaces that already include other visual liturgical arts, media art may further enrich the community's worship with a new creation, a moment of beauty that is "true to the complexity of life."[32] Beauty does not necessarily equate with the sights, sounds, and motion that are merely pleasant, nostalgic, or romantic. In the light of the Cross and the Resurrection, beauty shines out in media art that is authentic, genuine, and truthful. Protestant theologian Karl Barth speaks of beauty as that which "embraces death as well as life, fear as well as joy, what we might call the ugly as well as we might call the beautiful."[33] Janet Walton, professor of worship and the arts at Union Theological Seminary, reminds her students and readers that in worship, beauty expresses the "pain, frustration, and struggle as well as the promise of fullness of life."[34] Likewise, Don Saliers speaks of art in worship, and of worship itself, as necessarily containing permanent tensions between the visible and invisible, the audible and inaudible, the already and not yet, the desire and the act, the infinite and the finite. Beauty contains, Saliers writes, "permanent tensions."[35]

Media art in worship may reveal the beauty of human dignity even in the depths of degradation and destruction. Beauty can cause people to stop, to notice, to see perhaps for the first time something otherwise ignored. Images of individuals who are homeless, famished, and orphaned, or images of polluted rivers and clear-cut forests, are not necessarily "nice" pictures. Referring to the music videos created by members of Union-Congregational UCC Church, one worshiper explained: "Sometimes, they are pictures that you might not necessarily want to look at. They remind you of things . . . like children in the Third World countries that are hungry. You might not necessarily like to think about that, but it gets your mind going."[36]

Beauty in art of any kind calls on those who perceive it to open their eyes and hearts, to enter into the ambiguity and infinite mystery of life. Of course, in the creation of liturgical media art that is "something beautiful for God," to use Mother Teresa's expression, liturgical aesthetics and media aesthetics need to be learned and practiced. Not all that one creates with the intention of providing beauty succeeds at that level. "The visual arts, like all others, can be trivial and, with respect to religious content or style, banal. But they can also offer profound insight."[37] So, too, media arts. "Beauty illuminates," as Andrew Greeley succinctly puts it.[38] Consequently, it is a worthy endeavor to create media that provides beauty within worship. But to evaluate whether media in worship provides beauty, those creating and evaluating it must develop some aesthetic sense, the focus of the third critical framework.

Framework III: Aesthetics for Liturgical Media Art

"Aesthetics" is a word that may not resonate with many people. Nothing substantive may come to mind upon hearing it. Yet, whether they associate the word with their actions, people attend to aesthetics frequently throughout their day. Whenever people decorate a room, choose a car, set a table, make dinner, pick a CD to enjoy or a TV program to watch, select clothing, or take a snapshot, they are making aesthetic decisions. They are making choices related not only to function but also to color, flavor, spatial relationships, physical arrangements, patterns, sounds, style, line, fit, and many other aesthetic criteria. Such decisions consider multiple factors and may apply to an immediate circumstance or to something that takes place over time. For example, people's aesthetic choices lead them to plant their garden in a certain pattern with flowers of particular colors, shapes, and sizes that will bloom at anticipated times of the year so that they can enjoy the visual "orchestration" of their garden with each growing season. Church leaders need to take at least as much care in making aesthetic decisions regarding the integration of media into worship and the worship environment.

1. Liturgical Aesthetics

An understanding of aesthetics is essential to the appropriate integration of media in worship. Aesthetics simply refers to what is erceptible, to what people can see, hear, touch, taste, and smell. It includes a sense for time, timing, rhythm, pacing, and tempo. As John Witvliet notes, "legitimate criteria for liturgical aesthetics arise out of reflection on the nature of liturgy itself. Method in liturgical aesthetics consists of reflections about liturgy, on *liturgical experience.*"[39]

Media in worship that would qualify as liturgical media art must be developed for and evaluated within a particular context, what Frank Burch Brown calls an "aesthetic milieu."[40] All that can be perceived within the space and within the event of the overall worship context, including its worshiping community, comprises a church's aesthetic milieu. Leaders using Framework I to analyze the context for their use of media in worship will quickly find themselves in the thick of liturgical aesthetic analyses, whether or not they realize it. For, the basic question of liturgical aesthetics is simply this: Is media in worship *appropriate, fitting,* and *integral* to this community's ritual actions, interactions, liturgical arts, and worship space?

The aesthetic integration of media within worship affects the dynamic flow of the worship event itself. How would media—where it is placed within the service, in what space it is displayed, when it is used—affect the timing, pace, rhythm, and choreography of the actions and interactions typical of that ritual form? All of these factors influence worshipers' aesthetic experience of their service.

An example of decision making related to liturgical aesthetics is the complex issue of where and how media is projected or displayed. Specialists who recommend the size of media screens for any viewing space follow a standard formula to calculate the right size based on the distance of the furthest worshiper from the screen, the kind of screen, and the angles of vision involved. Various other priorities, however, may dictate the size of media projections or displays. Media research has confirmed that the larger the screen, the greater the physiological effect its content has on those who watch it.[41] The size of any projection or display within a space needs to be evaluated liturgically and aesthetically, not just technically. Pertinent questions include: What are the proportions, scale, and locations of video projection or display in relationship to the overall liturgical space and to the gathered assembly? Is projected media a major, supportive, or minor element in the space? Is the projection dominant or subordinate to other visual elements of worship? Have screens been positioned wherever their placement seems practical and technically feasible, regardless of how they look or function for the worshipers? Is the projector powerful enough to deal with ambient light from natural sunlight? (Outside light can wash out images on a screen and make them difficult to see.) Does the screen really need to be on and active all the time? If so, why? What is on the screen when liturgical content is not being projected? (Some churches create a wallpaper graphic whose color matches the surrounding walls so that the screen seems to disappear when it is not needed. Other churches create a graphic whose color is in keeping with the liturgical season.)

Screens that have not been given an aesthetically designed frame (either through a colored border or drapery) and are displayed in their raw state with black edges showing, make an otherwise aesthetically pleasing space look industrial and ugly. Such screens may be necessary during an experimental stage or in a rented space, but once a final placement decision is made screens should complement the space, that is, be aesthetically integral as part of the environment.

Aesthetic decisions about these many matters have liturgical consequences, both positive and negative, and can speak volumes about a church's theological understanding of the role of media in worship. Is worship determining how media is used, or is media use dictating worship? The screen can become an idol that must be fed media all the time. Much is at stake in these decisions. Regardless of its artistic merits, media in worship must first be judged against the criteria of liturgical aesthetics. If, instead, media and its media aesthetics are more important, then those priorities may be a sign of a significant liturgical problem. Media may be driving the worship.

2. Media Aesthetics

Media aesthetics must also be factored into the assessment of what is projected or displayed. Since art, as understood in this essay, is a social practice, practitioners need to acquire skills, to learn their craft, and to appreciate the art's traditions and conventions; but they also need to meet certain aesthetic standards and then pass on those skills and standards to others. Art is a communal practice. Of course, expectations of the art of beginners are always different from those of master artists. Communities need master artists to help beginners' skills and art mature. Standards change with time and can vary from community to community. Standards of quality, for example, are typically communally and culturally set. What qualifies as art in some communities might be judged as kitsch in another community.

Just as decisions about media's integration require intentionality regarding liturgical aesthetics, decisions about the aesthetic qualities of the *media itself* also demand intentionality. Some aesthetics are common to all arts. Some art forms have additional aesthetic criteria that differentiate "good" from "bad" art of that form. Consider a graphic art form common in worship, the PowerPoint slide. Even with the help of provided templates, people can still put together poorly designed text slides and execute ineffectively timed slide changes. As media minister Tim Eason notes, just because someone can work with design software does not mean that person automatically has the artistic eye, the sense of timing, or the aesthetic training required to create a graphic that is aesthetically pleasing and effectively communicative.[42]

Currently, much graphic and photographic media prepared for inclusion in worship reflects the style of 1990s corporate presentation audiovisuals.[43] Worship is not a board meeting. Often, available media art for worship tends, stylistically, to have a very similar computer-generated, contemporary look, even when photos and video are involved. Most media-art-for-worship collections seem disconnected from religious visual arts of the ages.

In addition to developing the skills demanded by program software, those creating graphics for worship need to learn and to respect the basic rules of aesthetics for graphic and other visual arts. Amateurs who take lessons to improve their photographs discover quickly that *photographic aesthetics* involve composition, color, texture, scale and proportion, harmony and disharmony, balance and imbalance, symmetry and asymmetry, foreground and background, negative and positive space, and the overall integration or fragmentation of elements. *Graphic arts aesthetics* include working also with a recognition of the importance of contrast, alignment, color relationships, and repetition, as well as many other aesthetic elements. A sense for aesthetics can make the difference between a photo or graphic that communicates and one that irritates. A text slide with type that is too small to be easily read by those for whom it is intended does not encourage worshipers' participation. A poorly composed photograph or graphic may call attention to itself, rather than to its content.[44]

When people create video material for worship, they need an appreciation for the aesthetics of video production and arts. In addition to previously mentioned aesthetic criteria, basic *video aesthetics* include consideration of motion, rhythm, tempo, timing, repetition, flow, and careful use of sound and silence.

When creating media installation art for worship, church artists need to consider how a variety of art forms can combine to create an overall experience and how the design of the installation can encourage people's interaction within a three-dimensional space. Interactivity differentiates installation art from some other art forms. *Installation art aesthetics* may provide a good discipline for thinking about the worship event, because one could envision the entire worship space and all that happens in it as a form of installation art.

When performance arts—such as, music, drama, mime, dance, poetry or other oral readings—are combined with media arts and are integrated within worship, *performance aesthetics* related to each art apply. When appropriately integrated within a service, all the arts contribute to the overall effectiveness of the service in communicating the gospel message and to the possibility of media arts being among the liturgical arts that can provide beauty.

In sum, aesthetics from graphic, photographic, video production and art, installation art, and performance arts all potentially contribute to whether media in worship is perceived as aesthetically engaging of worshipers' senses and sacramental imaginations.

3. Liturgical Media Aesthetics

If liturgical aesthetics do not come first in aesthetic decision making, a church's media may be just media *in* worship and not media *of* worship. By the standards of media aesthetics, a church's media may be *media art*, yet not be *liturgical media art*, because it fails to serve worship as an integral element. In short, liturgical aesthetics and media aesthetics go hand in hand in the creation of liturgical media art. When they do, churches are operating from the perspective of a new form of aesthetics: liturgical media aesthetics.

Framework IV: Issues of Ethics and Justice

Ethical and justice issues related to media in worship are many, some obvious and some less so. They include living within a church's financial means and not overextending for the sake of the latest and greatest in media technology. They involve having just relationships with all who contribute to a church's media ministry and with all producers and artists whose work may be used. Justice also involves a variety of issues related to diversity and inclusion. Church leaders would do well to perform a regular examination of conscience in these areas.

1 & 2. Responsible resource allocation and living wages

In regard to resources—financial and human—church leaders need to be wise stewards. Responsible management of funds dedicated to media purchases may mean resisting the pressure of salespeople, a form of moderation Quentin Schultze calls "Technological Stewardship": "The safest way to address technology-related costs is to practice reasonable moderation within the context of excellence—not perfection. Many consultants will advise that a church should spend as much as it can afford on presentational technologies to avoid disappointing performance and the need to replace equipment in the near future. In most worship spaces, however, higher-end equipment is unnecessary."[45] Small congregations can carry on for a very long time with borrowed media equipment and volunteer talent. Often, this kind of low-cost experimentation is the best way to explore the possibilities of media in worship and to help those directly involved and those in the worshiping community gradually to come to a clearer sense of what is media *of* liturgy versus simply media *in* liturgy. Moreover by avoiding unnecessary equipment purchases, large churches can ensure that they have sufficient funds to pay just living wages to professional technical and media staff.

3. License and copyright permission

Ethical stewardship extends also to paying for original and copyrighted art and for the permission to use it. Churches of all sizes need to purchase music and media licenses and to educate all people involved about the importance of respecting and working within copyright law. The actual cost of purchasing licenses is based on church membership and is relatively inexpensive.[46] Eason and Bausch both provide guidelines on how to purchase licenses, seek permissions, and identify material on the Internet and elsewhere that is and is not copyrighted.[47]

4. Social justice issues

In addition to ethical concerns, the creation of media for worship raises social justice issues as well. In the first place, are social injustices even depicted? Does a church's media art give voice to the voiceless and demonstrate respect for those people whom society commonly shuns or treats with disdain? Are realities such as poverty, hunger, and environmental destruction confronted? Are images challenging, as well as comforting, to those who encounter them? Is the media art itself truthful and, as appropriate, even prophetic?

5, 6, & 7. Diversity in people, media art, and metaphors for God

What is shown on-screen is the result of local decision making. But imagery must be local *and* universal. In examining local media, leaders need to ask themselves: Over time, whose images are shown? Whose voices are heard? Do media segments represent only people who look like the church's members? Do they represent people from diverse cultures and races, as well as people who live with disabilities? Diversity in the imagery of peoples, places, genders, and ages should be a consistent goal of media ministry. Sensitizing media team members to issues of inclusion is an important task for church leaders. On a regular basis media ministers should examine their media art and ask, Who's missing? The power to create media art inherently includes the power to exclude other people, both from its creation and from their being represented in its imagery. It is very easy to fall back on creating media art that is safe and familiar and that reflects the people who create it. Who ultimately decides what media is integrated within worship? From whose point of view is liturgical media art created? Whether media ministers create custom-made media art, purchase it from a worship media vendor, or appropriate material and combine it into a new creation, they must ensure that imagery does justice to all of God's people and leaves none of them forever invisible.

Working from the common translation of "liturgy" as "the work of the people," a case can be made that media art for liturgy should also be the work of the people, not just that of a closed inner circle. How might the ministry be opened up? How could the circle-of-the-included become more fluid and permeable? Inclusion of those people who are typically excluded from liturgical ministry is one of the wonderful opportunities of this new media ministry. Everyone engaged in today's media cultures potentially has something to offer, whether through suggestions made in a brainstorming session or production of actual media art. In assessing the degree of inclusion in media ministry, local leaders can ask themselves: Who is welcomed in the creative process? Who qualifies as a contributing artist in this ministry? Is participation restricted based on age or membership criteria? Are people who live with disabilities, who are from another country, who have a different skin color, or who are economically disadvantaged invited to contribute to the creative process of the church's liturgical media art?

Furthermore, how inclusive is the process of determining what kinds of popular media, what languages, and what metaphors are incorporated into worship? Whose art and popular media is valued? Do scenes from movies of interest to women appear as frequently as those of interest to men (or vice versa)? Is recorded music that is used representative of the diversity of tastes and ages in your community? How gender-inclusive is the language used in the church's media? Are verbal and visual images of God consistently that of white males? How might the wider range of biblical and other metaphorical imagery of God be depicted? [48]

The four evaluative frameworks—overall worship context, functions of media, liturgical media aesthetics, and issues of ethics and justice—challenge local leaders to think critically when incorporating media into their worship life. Chapter 5 focuses particularly on how church leaders, using these four frameworks, might encourage the development of a new liturgical ministry in which liturgical media art has the chance to flourish.

Notes

1. These magazines began to target the needs of the church market in the mid- to late-1990s, as increasing numbers of medium-sized churches moved from simply having sound amplification systems to installing full-blown integrated computer-controlled media systems.

2. Don and Janet Beasley, "Jazzing Up Your Stage," *Technologies for Worship Magazine* (2003): 26, 28, 30. This magazine's website is http://www.tfwm.com.

3. John P. Whelan, "Lights! Camera! Worship!: Flat Irons Community Church, Lafayette, Colorado," *Church Production Magazine* 5, no. 3 (2003): 16, 20–21, 38. This magazine's website is http://www.churchproduction.com.

4. "About Vision," *Vision* 1, no. 1 (2003): 4. Produced by Fowler, Inc., a company that provides churches with media in worship consultation, system design, installation, and training. Their website is http://www.fowlerdesign-group.com. Their *Vision* magazine can be accessed at http://www.vision-mag.com.

5. Kellian Schneider and Jim Miller, "From 36 to 1,900 in 18 months!: How Journey Church is Reaching a City," *Vision* 1, no. 1 (2003): 8–12.

6. The magazines' websites are http://www.worshipleader.com and http://www.faithworks.com.

7. Among the growing number of for-purchase media-art-for-worship websites are http://www.highwayvideo.com, http://www.lumicon.org, http://www.midnightoilproductions.com, http://www.worshipfilms.com, and http://www.worshipphotos.com. Church media artists freely share their work with other churches via a special section of downloadable "shareware" media art on the website of http://www.churchmedia.net, the website of Tim Eason and colleagues dedicated to training church media ministers. Eason has produced *Media Ministry Made Easy: A Practical Guide to Visual Communication* (Nashville, TN: Abingdon Press, 2003), a book including a DVD with demonstration examples, and usable sample graphics, videos, and PowerPoint presentations.

8. "Embracing innovation to enrich ministry," Cokesbury Software Resources 2004 (product catalog).

9. To see a video streaming sample of worship and how this church uses media for presentation of lyrics, go to the Menlo Park Presbyterian Church website http://www.mppcfamily.org.

10. Handt Hanson, (ELCA Prince of Peace Church, worship and music team leader, Burnsville, MN), phone interview by author, March 2004.

11. The Church of the Apostles website is http://www.apostleschurch.org.

12. See Eileen Crowley-Horak, "Testing the Fruits: Aesthetics as Applied to Liturgical Media Art," (dissertation, Union Theological Seminary, 2002).

Available from Proquest Information and Learning. http://proquest.com/ products_umi/dissertations/. ProQuest ID no. 726435071, publication no. AAT 3048887, ISBN 9780493632179.

13. Ibid., 105–6.

14. Ibid., 120–26. Psalm refrain taken from "Evening Prayer," *Lutheran Book of Worship* (Minneapolis, MN: Augsburg Publishing; Philadelphia, PA: Board of Publication, Lutheran Church in America, 1978), 145–46.

15. Description of Paul Tillich's categories as provided by Joan Carter, "The Role of the Arts in Worship," in *Postmodern Worship and The Arts*, ed. Doug Adams and Michael Moynahan (San Jose, CA: Resource Publications, 2002), 77.

16. Incident report in focus group facilitated by author, Union-Congregational UCC Church, Waupun, WI, November 10, 2001.

17. Nicolas de Oliveira, Nicola Oxley, and Michael Petry, *Installation Art* (London: Thames and Hudson, 1994), 13.

18. David A. Ross and Peter Sellers, *Bill Viola* (New York: Whitney Museum of American Art, 1998), 20.

19. Ibid., 14.

20. Ibid., 124.

21. Ibid., 102.

22. Ibid., 27.

23. Rev. Dr. Troy Messenger, (Union Theological Seminary, James Chapel director of worship, New York City), discussion with author. The service referenced took place in May 2001.

24. John Dykstra Eusden and John H. Westerhoff, III, *Sensing Beauty: Aesthetics, the Human Spirit, and the Church* (Cleveland, OH: United Church Press, 1998), 27.

25. Elaine Scarry, *On Beauty and Being Just* (Princeton, NJ: Princeton University Press, 1999), 115.

26. A term of John Shea's from his essay, "The Second Naiveté: Approach to a Pastoral Problem," *Concilium* 81 (1973): 110, cited in Mark Searle, "Liturgy as Metaphor," *Worship* 55, no. 2 (1981): 101.

27. In advising on how to introduce a new form of art into a service, Union Theological Seminary's professor of worship, Janet Walton, urges "meticulous attention to its integration": "All symbolic forms require space and time for interaction. Too many powerful symbols in succession can be overwhelming, even deadening, just as too few or none at all can leave a great lacuna. Care must be exercised to assess the proper arrangement and rhythm. Often balance is difficult." Janet R. Walton, *Art in Worship: A Vital Connection* (Wilmington, DE: Michael Glazier, 1988), 114.

28. Nicholas Wolterstorff, *Art in Action: Toward a Christian Aesthetic* (Carlisle, UK: Solway, 1997), 22; (Grand Rapids, MI: William B. Eerdmans Publishing, 1980).

29. Eusden and Westerhoff, *Sensing Beauty*, 5.

30. See William A. Dyrness, *Visual Faith: Art, Theology, and Worship in Dialogue* (Grand Rapids, MI: Baker Books, 2001) or, for a shorter treatment of the subject see his essay, "Reclaiming Art for Worship," *Theology, News and Notes* (2001), available at http://www.fuller.edu/news/pubs/tnn/2001_oct.htm. Robin M. Jensen, "The Arts in Protestant Worship," *Theology Today* 58, no. 3 (2001): 359–68. Sally Morgenthaler, "A Tangible God," in *Worship Evangelism: Inviting Unbelievers into the Presence of God* (Grand Rapids, MI: Zondervan Publishing, 1995/1999), 134–35.

31. Scarry, *On Beauty and Being Just*, 11.

32. Eusden and Westerhoff, *Sensing Beauty*, 89.

33. Quoted in Jeremy S. Begbie, *Voicing Creation's Praise: Towards a Theology of the Arts* (Edinburgh: T & T Clark, 1991), 224.

34. Walton, *Art in Worship*, 60.

35. Don E. Saliers, "Proclamation Through the Arts: Poet, Painter, Music-Maker," in *Lifting Up Jesus Christ Yesterday, Today, and Forever: Proceedings of Worship 2000 Jubilee* (Chicago, IL: Evangelical Lutheran Church in America, 2001), 28.

36. Carrie Bruins, (Union-Congregational UCC Church member, Waupun, WI), interview with author, November 2001.

37. Saliers, "Proclamation Through the Arts," 5.

38. Andrew M. Greeley, "The Apologetics of Beauty: Liturgy should be enjoyable—Pope John Paul II," *America* 183, no. 7 (2000): 8–13, 14.

39. John. D. Witvliet, "Toward a Liturgical Aesthetics: An Interdisciplinary Review of Aesthetic Theory," *Liturgy Digest* 3, no. 1 (1996): 73. Emphasis added.

40. ". . . the aesthetic milieu . . . comprises everything in focal or subsidiary awareness that, within a particular context, is either immediately or mediately aesthetic in effect." Frank Burch Brown, *Religious Aesthetics: A Theological Study of Making and Meaning* (Princeton, NJ: Princeton University Press, 1989), 55.

41. ". . . there is some compelling empirical evidence that, despite the fact that mediated presentation provides a limited reproduction of nonmediated experience, media users do react to filmed and televised presentations in some of the same ways that they react to nonmediated events, objects and people . . . These responses are here termed *direct* because they suggest that viewers are responding not only to the *portrayal* of events but directly to the events and objects themselves, as if the events and objects were immediately present in the viewing room." Matthew Lombard, "Direct Responses to People

on the Screen: Television and Personal Space" *Communications Research* 22, no. 3 (1995): 288–324, at 288–89.

42. Eason, *Media Ministry Made Easy,* ibid.

43. Len Wilson and Jason Moore, *Digital Storytellers: The Art of Communicating the Gospel in Worship* (Nashville, TN: Abingdon Press, 2002), 16–19.

44. Training in photographic and graphic aesthetics is often available at local community colleges and art schools.

45. Schultze, *High-Tech Worship,* 79.

46. See, for example, the Christian Video Licensing Inc. website for more information, http://www.cvli.org.

47. See Michael G. Bausch, "Concerning Copyright," in *Silver Screen, Sacred Story: Using Multimedia in Worship* (Bethesda, MD: Alban Institute, 2002), 90–95; Eason, "Copyrights," in *Media Ministry,* 69–75.

48. For inspiration on the great variety of names (and thus images and metaphors) for God, see the work of theologian Elizabeth A. Johnson, especially "Many Names," *She Who Is* (New York: Crossroad, 1993), 117–20, and "Naming God She," *Princeton Seminary Bulletin* 22, no. 2 (2001): 134–49. Cf. Thomas Aquinas, *Summa Contra Gentiles* I, Chapter 34 [4], trans. Anton C. Pegis, (Garden City, NY: Hanover House, 1955): ". . . we see the necessity for giving God many names . . . The names by which we signify His perfection must be diverse . . ."

5 A Model for Liturgical Media Ministry: Communal Co-Creation

On a vendor's website, an article entitled "How to Use Multimedia in Your Church Worship Service" begins: "It's not as hard as you might think! With a minimum investment, a strategy for implementation, and a willingness to get creative, you can be on your way to successfully using multimedia in no time. . . . The place to start is with the right equipment."[1] As should be evident by now, that is exactly the *wrong* place to start. Liturgy always should be the starting point. More specifically, since liturgy is the work of the people giving praise and thanks to God, people should be the starting point, not technology.

For those seeking to begin their own media ministry, web resources and literature on media in worship could easily throw them off track, because the dominant model of media ministry is a production crew model. In a production crew model, the focus of the media ministry is to train church members to operate cameras, to work with worship production software, or to help with some other aspects of video production. Volunteers are welcome to be part of the production or media projection team, but they are typically not members of the creative or decision-making team, except in small churches.

The production crew model of media ministry is a very limited view of what is possible for those who participate. I propose an alternative approach in which the emphasis is on *ministry*, as a liturgical ministry, rather than on the media or its production. This model begins with liturgy, includes all the faithful in the creative process, and encourages the creation of locally produced liturgical media art. I call this model for liturgical media ministry "Communal Co-Creation." Here is the vision in a nutshell: Communal Co-Creation is a local creative, artistic, and spiritual process that welcomes people of all ages to be involved in the evaluation, creation, and reception of media in worship. Communal Co-Creation is a process, not a product or a program.

It is within the context of Communal Co-Creation that the four evaluative frameworks presented in chapter 4 are most useful. This evaluative process can be implemented in a variety of ways, but it must be customized to the needs and resources of a local community. Churches differ widely in whether, when, how, and to what degree they should introduce new media into their worship. Some church leaders may decide to experiment with media at a particular service or during a particular liturgical season and then stop and evaluate their experience before proceeding further.[2] The evaluative frameworks can help them in that task. Some church leaders may choose to go slowly and gradually incorporate media in worship, while others may decide to jump in and buy media equipment and quickly establish a media team. Regardless of how a church chooses, or how it has already chosen, to introduce new media into their worship, the evaluative frameworks provided in Chapter 4 can help church leaders and members view this new ministry *liturgically*, *inclusively*, and *critically*.

Communal Co-Creation: A Process

How does a church begin to use media in worship? The idea may come from a minister who has been to a conference, from a church elder who sees media as a way to attract teens or the unchurched, from lay people who have experienced media in churches elsewhere, or from teens in the youth ministry. Somebody says, "Maybe we should consider using media in our worship." It is at this very early point in a church's discernment process that the working vocabulary and four evaluative frameworks come into play. These tools can help a church decide whether this new media and new ministry are appropriate for their circumstances.

Regardless of what may trigger deliberations on media in worship, church leaders can begin by inviting other members to form a discernment group to explore the possibilities. The group might include the pastor, other ministers, members of the worship committee and music ministry, lay leaders, other church members with relevant backgrounds or experience, young adults, teens, and others who may simply be interested in the possibility and have responded to church announcements that "all are welcome." Of course, any gathering of church folks addressing this topic might include those who see peril, as well as those who see positive possibilities. If so, good. An honest, healthy discussion can result if participants begin in prayer and agree to allow themselves not only to be educated along the way but also to be open to each other and to the Holy Spirit.

Tools already provided in this essay can help reduce miscommunication and misunderstandings even at this early discernment stage. Whoever is facilitating the exploratory discussions could provide all participants with an introduction to the working vocabulary presented in chapter 1 and give a brief synopsis of the century-long history of media in Christian worship. With that background in place, participants could begin to consider their overall worship context through the foundational evaluative questions presented in Framework I. They would then address how the introduction of media might affect their community's worship given their particular forms of worship, the liturgical actions typically involved, the people who comprise the community, and the overall worship environment. While they may seem to be dealing only with very practical liturgical and community matters, they are really engaged in a form of theological reflection:

> The sense of the faithful . . . is a supernatural sense of the faith given to the whole people by the Holy Spirit. (Dogmatic Constitution on the Church 12). Theological reflection is one way the faithful exercise their sense of the faith. It may not have the precision and crispness of the traditional notes in scholarly manuals, but it is a more ancient and trustworthy guide to the meaning of tradition. And it turns the experience into a thing of beauty.[3]

To gain a greater sense of the faithful on this topic, leaders might recruit additional people and form several exploratory groups to go through this same discernment process and to contribute their ideas nd questions to these early "Should we?" discussions. Based on these preliminary reflections, church leaders decide whether to proceed.

If the decision is, "We'll look into this some more," then Framework II assists in this next step. It describes the many functions media might serve in worship. In reflecting on these functions, participants in this discernment process are reminded that neither all liturgies (Framework I) nor all media in worship (Framework II) functions in the same way. Being able to make such distinctions is an important factor in productive group discernment on this topic. In working through Framework II especially, participants might find that their imaginations become stimulated by examples and begin to envision how media might function in their worship. If these discussions have been announced and are open and inclusive, the parish grapevine should now be abuzz with the subject. Good. The more people talk about their liturgy and what media might or might not contribute to it, the sooner they will begin to develop critical thinking skills needed for Communal Co-Creation.

To approach discernment as a communal process opens participation in this liturgical ministry to all and demonstrates that this ministry is inclusive. In most churches using media today, only a limited circle of staff and church members is involved in discerning whether to proceed with media in worship—and a limited circle of people serve in media ministry itself. In a similar way, participation in liturgical ministries may be limited to the ordained or to those with particular training, skills, and gifts. In contrast, the beauty of media ministry following this Communal Co-Creation model is that everyone interested can contribute in some way. They already have what it takes: experience with liturgy, media, and life. Attaining the technical skills and obtaining the equipment is important, but it is a secondary part of the process.

How might this process be structured organizationally once a decision is made to try media in worship? At the center of the process of Communal Co-Creation is a core group of people who are highly interested in reflecting upon and creating media for worship and who are equally committed to recruiting other people to create and to evaluate media for worship. The mission of the core group includes outreach, especially to those usually not invited into liturgical ministry. For example, this process can provide a wonderful reason and opportunity to welcome artists back into faith communities. Instead of a closed circle, liturgical media ministry has permeable boundaries. By design it would have many openings through which people could enter the process as they were interested and able. At various points, through those openings might walk film and TV buffs, computer techies, teenage animators, music fans and musicians, photographers and other media folk, poets and musicians, graphic artists and art teachers, people who love to organize and coordinate, amateurs and professionals in a craft or art, and imaginative people of all sorts. Moreover, in Communal Co-Creation people need not be physically present at meetings to participate. The speaker phone offers one avenue for remote participation of those who cannot attend sessions. E-mail or mail correspondence is another way someone can participate in the media ministry's brainstorming. A worship team in Ohio benefited from the input of a church member who contributed by mail from his prison cell.[4] The potential benefits of inclusion are great. Whenever and wherever people reflect on how Scripture and worship relate to their lives and are invited to contribute their thoughts and talents, they participate in a new form of spiritual practice. Those who have had this opportunity usually report that they are much more attentive and engaged when they participate in liturgy.

Practically speaking, how might these diverse people contribute? In diverse ways. Some members might ultimately choose to be "regulars." Other individuals might be recruited as creative freelancers to bring their gifts to the process for a particular service or season. Still others who enter this ministry could be members of church groups, such as a men's group or social ministry committee. Groups or ministries might ask to enter this artistic, creative process so that they could produce media art for a liturgical season, a particular feast, or liturgical occasion.

How might people be invited into the process? Person-to-person and through every communications medium the church has available. In Protestant churches whose worship is theme-based, the church bulletin might note that a series on a particular topic (e.g., the Ten Commandments, Women in the Bible, The Cross) is in the making and that members are welcome to join in discussions about creative use of media related to that topic. For communities following an official order of worship, the core group might follow the practice common to many worship committees. Many weeks or even months in advance, the core group reads and reflects upon the upcoming liturgical season: the lectionary readings, the prayers, and other ritual elements specific to those services.[5] The core group makes known that these are not closed sessions. For Catholic, Anglican, Lutheran, and other churches whose Sunday Scripture is already set out in a lectionary, an invitation could go out to all members, even to a local community through a brief notice in the newspaper: "This Advent we will be reading these passages from Isaiah and Luke. We invite you to read them and come to an open discussion where we will reflect on movies, films, or music that you think speak to these passages or that suggest the very mood and meaning of Advent."

Additionally, the core group might sponsor a retreat using media as the catalyst for spiritual reflection in preparation for upcoming liturgical seasons or feast days. The lead media ministers might approach a specific group in the church for a special project. For All Saints Day, for example, members might reflect with and commission a confirmation or youth group to produce their own talking, moving media version of the ancient practice of liturgical art featuring universal and local saints.

When people gather for these shared reflections in Communal Co-Creation, their conversation might sound like that of a worship committee or a music ministry committee. (Of course, members of liturgical media ministry need to be collaborating closely with people in other liturgical ministries, and the core group should make sure participants from those ministries are regularly invited into the media ministry reflection process.) Inspired by prayerful reflections on liturgy, media, and life, participants brainstorm and discover how media art might bring something otherwise unavailable to worship. Film or TV buffs might recall scenes that speak to the metaphors or themes under discussion. Music fans might recall a popular or religious song. Someone very interested in exploring and keeping up-to-date on available media art for worship (that can be downloaded and/or purchased over the Internet) might suggest graphic art, a video vignette, or a media environmental background they have noted in their research. Still other participants skilled with a still or video camera might volunteer to create media art especially designed for a service or season. Or the group might identify a freelance producer or team who could bring an idea to life as media art. Brainstorming at this stage should be a playful process in which nothing is rejected out of hand. However, at some point the core group needs to make decisions on which ideas or media art to pursue. But they need not flounder at that decision-making stage. They can evaluate any media proposals that church members ultimately put on the table by using Framework III, liturgical media aesthetics, as well as by considering the evaluative criteria from the other three frameworks.

Once any proposed media art is in hand—whether homemade, appropriated, or purchased— the core group, including key ministers or preachers, needs to make a final decision based on all four evaluative frameworks, including issues of ethics and justice presented in Framework IV. Is this media art, as we envision its use in our worship, appropriate, fitting, and integral? All four evaluative frameworks ultimately move church leaders to ask this question. It cannot be dodged. The frameworks, though, are on hand to help answer it. (As evaluative and diagnostic tools they can be useful throughout the process: in the planning stage, in the production and selection stage, in diagnosing problems when media does not work, and in testing the liturgical experience against the plan afterward.)

If at the final decision-making stage the answer is, "No, this media art will not work for this service," that does not mean it cannot still serve the church. While the media art might not be appropriate for liturgy, it might still be useful in other parish settings, such as religious education, Scripture study, or small faith-sharing groups. The media art might work on the church's website. In short, what is produced but rejected may still have life as something that prepares or helps worshipers reflect on some aspect of a service, season, or ministry. It might also be appropriate for use on another occasion.

In one Chicago parish, St. Bede the Venerable Church, each member of a class of seventh graders produced a PowerPoint slide meditation on families for their liturgy celebrating International Day of Families. The media art of just two of the seventy-three students was ultimately selected for that service. However, all students gained in multiple ways from the experience. In the creative brainstorming and production process, every child who produced media art became deeply engaged in reflecting on the theme, a special song on families, and the Scripture of that liturgy. Many of them called on members of their families to collaborate in their creation. They learned the basic skills of producing a media meditation. Each student's work ultimately was shown to the whole class. When the religious education director invited students to be part of the next year's liturgy planning team, about half the class signed on.[6]

Media producers and artists, regardless of their age, make themselves vulnerable by offering their talents to create media for worship. Thus they need to know from the start that the art they create is communal art, tribal art, and that it will ultimately be judged on the communal standards of liturgical media aesthetics. Whether or not their media art is used in worship, they need to be properly praised and thanked for their gift. If their work is not used at all, they deserve a compassionate, sensitively-worded evaluation based on the criteria of the frameworks, not on decision-makers' personal aesthetic or taste preferences. If at the final decision-making stage the core group says, "Yes, let's use this media," then the media ministers must work closely with other liturgical ministers to ensure that the media art is gracefully integrated into the service.

Communal Co-Creation does not stop at this point. The process also calls for evaluation of media in worship after its use. Church leaders can invite different groups of worshipers to reflect on the liturgy and the media art. When they are so invited, they are being welcomed into the liturgical reflection process called mystagogy, reflection on the one Mystery of God encountered in that liturgy. The insights and suggestions that are stirred in the course of these discussions can be fed back to the core group. And the process spirals back once again, just as liturgical planning always does, as the core group welcomes people to reflect on another service or season.

If the preceding scenario seems wildly idealistic, know that this model is based on field research in the experiences of actual faith communities who developed their own version of Communal Co-Creation, though they most likely would not have used that term for the process. The possibilities for Communal Co-Creation, here presented, come from the experience of churches working within their own liturgical tradition and its orders of worship. Although one church with a liturgical media ministry has 10,000 members, other churches that have successfully created an inclusive, creative process for developing media for their worship have had only 100 to 350 members.[7]

What does it take to develop and sustain an inclusive, open model as envisioned for this liturgical ministry? Foundational is the belief that liturgy *is* the work of the people who are participating in the ministry of Christ. Unless leaders are committed to an open and collaborative process, though, Communal Co-Creation will never happen. Joseph Gelineau writes poignantly about the temptation of church leaders to hold on too tightly to liturgy. Leaders need to let go, he says, and toss the ball of responsibility to people in the assembly. Who knows, the people might even catch it. And if they do, they might realize *they* are the real players in the game.[8] When worshipers do discover that they are all performers in their liturgical celebrations, they enter into what Janet Walton has called Holy Play.[9]

Formation for Communal Co-Creation

In order for a community to sustain Communal Co-Creation as an ongoing process, church leaders must commit to ongoing formation. Formation in liturgical media ministers, whether members of a church's staff or volunteers is critical to the spiritual health of these ministers and of a church's media ministry. No matter the number of people participating in liturgical media ministry, church leaders are responsible for seeing that these ministers receive liturgical, biblical, theological, spiritual, and ethical catecheses. How else can they and the church's media art mature over time? The pastor does not necessarily have to be the one to offer this formation, but he or she does have the responsibility to see that others help these ministers grow in their understanding of worship, scripture, theology, and ethics so that these ministers develop a deeper spiritual and theological foundation for their ministry.

Formation also includes aesthetic training. This need provides an ideal opportunity for church leaders to reach out to local visual, graphic, computer and media artists, art teachers, professional photographers, videographers, and other artists. These experts may already be members of the church; they may just need to be invited to contribute. Churches may also locate help in their media ministers' aesthetic formation by calling on those who are teaching art and media in local high schools, community colleges, technical schools, and universities. Organizations of local artists are also good sources for leads to potential teachers who can help media ministers develop their aesthetic senses and artistic skills. Of course, media ministers also need ongoing technical training and updating as software and equipment changes and as new members join this ministry. Often, once equipment has been installed and demonstrated, volunteer media ministers teach themselves or each other how to work with equipment or software. However, churches would profit in the long run from spending less money on media equipment and more on training their media ministers.

Also essential for participation in Communal Co-Creation is learning how to do theological reflection. Church leaders and media ministers will find theological reflection necessary in every aspect of this undertaking. As "a creative task employing imagination and freedom and leaving the final results open-ended," writes Robert Kinast, "theological reflection resembles a work of art more than an intellectual exercise, and it appeals more to a sense of aesthetics than to the criteria of scientific rationality."[10] In the case of Communal Co-Creation, it can be a work of art that results in a work of art.

The frameworks discussed above provide a model for theological reflection, in the specific context of a liturgical media ministry, that is best used in conjunction with other forms of theological reflection.[11] Doing theological reflection of any kind inevitably leads participants down a common path. Robert Kinast describes this path as involving a "deceptively simple threefold movement." "It begins with the lived experience of those doing the reflection [within their social and cultural context]; it correlates this experience with the sources of the Christian tradition; and it draws out practical implications for Christian living."[12] Media ministers are doing a form of "local theology."[13]

Theology underpins Communal Co-Creation, conceptually and practically. All along the way, participants in this process benefit by asking themselves, "Where is God in all of this?" Unmoored from their tradition's theology, a church's media for their worship may not be reflective of their tradition's beliefs about worship, about God, about humanity, or about all of God's creation. Without a christology and liturgical theology that, like Jesus, privileges inclusion, media ministry may become one more instance of exclusion in the church. Grounded in an ecclesiology of mutual relation and right relationship based on Jesus' own treatment of people and hospitality to all, local creation of liturgical media art can instead become a process and ministry in which all are truly welcome. Acting on the very belief that the Spirit moves throughout Communal Co-Creation, a community lives from a deep confidence based on its pneumatology. Since this liturgical ministry is designed to constantly reach out to both church insiders and outsiders, it encourages reflection on missiology.

As may be obvious by now, a theology of grace is foundational to Communal Co-Creation. In the course of theological reflection, participants in the Communal Co-Creation of media become more attuned to grace in "the things of the world," as Anglican theologian John Macquarrie puts it, in ways that allow those things to become "so transparent that in them and through them we know God's presence and activity in our very midst, and so experience his grace."[14] Karl Rahner, who wrote extensively on grace, offers a theology particularly pertinent to the creation and reception of liturgical media art. Grace, understood as God's Self-Communication, abounds. In fact, says Rahner, we are drenched in grace and, as creatures who are *Imago Dei* (Latin, "Image of God") we have the potential and capacity to receive that grace (the supernatural existential). God's grace, so understood, is operative as a constitutive part of every human being, in every creative act of self-transcendence. Since God's Self-Communication is not limited to one privileged form of communication, in today's media cultures it follows that God's grace can be experienced via today's media ("the Church sees these media as 'gifts of God'"[15]).

Rahner's own theology of art rose out of his theology of grace. Art, he wrote, is a life-giving primordial word:

> In every primordial word there is signified a piece of reality in which a door is mysteriously opened for us into the unfathomable depths of true reality in general. The transition from the individual to the infinite in infinite movement, which is called by thinkers the transcendence of the spirit, itself belongs to the content of that primordial word. That is why it is more than a mere word: it is the soft music of the infinite movement of the spirit and of love for God, which begins with some small thing of this earth, which is seemingly the only thing meant by the word.[16]

The hope and vision of Communal Co-Creation is that the church may develop liturgical media art that rises to the level of being a "primordial word." Over time, through Communal Co-Creation, faith communities can come to identify and create "some small thing" out of which wafts "the soft music of the infinite movement of the spirit and of love for God." As they do, they are part of the church's crafting of a new liturgical art for worship in the midst of today's and tomorrow's media culture. "Thus says the Lord . . . I am about to do a new thing; now it springs forth, do you not perceive it?" (Isa 43:16a, 19a). During the last century, this "new thing" that is liturgical media art and ministry has taken root. It has yet to blossom fully. Its early fruits are still delicate and will only come to maturity with wise pastoral care and communal tending. How it may nourish God's people in the twenty-first century is a story yet to be written.

Notes

1. "How To Use Multimedia In Your Church Worship Service," http:// www.worshipfilms.com/getting-started.htm (10 March 2004).

2. This is the process Rev. Michael G. Bausch describes in his book, *Silver Screen: Sacred Story: Using Multimedia in Worship* (Silver Springs, MD: Alban Institute: 2002), as the approach he took in his own community, Union-Congregational UCC Church in Waupun, WI.

3. Robert L. Kinast, "Experiencing the Tradition Through Theological Reflection," *New Theology Review* 8, no. 1 (1995): 6.

4. Example from Pastor Kent Wilson, Trinity Lutheran Church, Willard, OH.

5. See, for example, the process outlined in Yvonne Cassa and Joanne Sanders, *Groundwork: Planning Liturgical Seasons* (Chicago, IL: Liturgy Training Publications, 1988); or annual editions of *Sourcebook for Sundays and Seasons* from Liturgy Training Publication, or *Sundays and Seasons* from Augsburg Press. Core team leaders could adapt the group brainstorming model that Edward Foley offers to preachers that engages the assembly as subjects of the preaching and involves members of the congregation directly in the preparation—and evaluation—of the homily. See Exercise 6 in Edward Foley, *Preaching Basics: A Model and a Method* (Chicago: Liturgy Training Publications, 1998) based upon a suggestion in the USCCB document *Fulfilled In Your Hearing: The Homily in the Sunday Assembly* (Washington D.C.: US Catholic Conference, 1982).

6. Diane Stephens, "Incorporating Media Art into Youth Worship: A Celebration of International Day of Families," (unpublished manuscript, May 2005).

7. Among the communities whose practices have inspired elements of my vision of Communal Co-Creation are these: the Catholic Community of the

Good Shepherd, Cincinnati, OH; Church of the Apostles, Seattle, WA; St. Joseph Church, Roseburg, OR; Scottsdale Congregational United Church of Christ, AZ; Trinity Lutheran Church, Willard, OH; and Union-Congregational UCC Church, Waupun, WI.

8. Joseph Gelineau, "The Symbols of Christian Initiation," in *Becoming A Catholic Christian Today*, ed. William Reedy (New York: Sadlier, 1979), 190–94. I am grateful to Janet Walton for sharing Gelineau's vision.

9. Janet R. Walton, "Improvisation and Imagination: Holy Play," *Worship* 75, no. 4 (2001): 290–304.

10. Kinast, "Experiencing the Tradition," 15.

11. From the start, a pastoral team and church members may engage in a ministerial style of reflection that helps them decide whether to even attempt the integration of media into their worship. They might turn to the work of James D. Whitehead and Evelyn Eaton Whitehead for guidance on the method of theological reflection most appropriate for dealing with complex issues and resolving conflicts in a collaborative endeavor. James D. and Evelyn E. Whitehead, *Method in Ministry*, rev. ed. (Kansas City: Sheed and Ward, 1995). They might look to the Whiteheads' model for collaborative ministry for help in "embracing the risk of collaboration" so important to this communal process. Evelyn Eaton Whitehead and James D. Whitehead, *The Promise of Partnership: A Model for Collaborative Ministry* (Lincoln, NE: iUniverse.com, 2000; originally published New York: Harper Collins, 1991), 3. Once having made the decision to go forward with the incorporation of media in their worship, church leaders and members might employ the methods of Patricia O'Connell Killen and John de Beer. They offer various methods of reflecting on experience, scripture, theology, tradition, and resources from the culture (including art and literature) that can be helpful to media ministers throughout the creative process: "Theological reflection is the process of seeking meaning that relies on the rich heritage of our Christian tradition as a primary source of wisdom and guidance. It presumes the profoundly incarnational (God present in human lives), providential (God caring for us), and revelatory (source of deepening knowledge of God and self) quality of human experience." They describe the art of theological reflection as "a movement toward insight." Patricia O'Connell Killen and John de Beer, *The Art of Theological Reflection* (New York: Crossroad, 1995), xi.

12. Robert L. Kinast, *What Are They Saying About Theological Reflection* (New York: Paulist Press, 2000), 1.

13. Robert Schreiter explains: "The three principal roots beneath the growth of local theology are gospel, church, and culture," in a dialectical relationship that gives "continuing attention to first one factor, and then another, leading to an ever-expanding awareness of the role and interaction of each of these

factors." In sum, "It takes the dynamic interaction of all of these roots—gospel, church and culture—with all they entail about identity and change, to have the makings of local theology." Robert J. Schreiter, *Constructing Local Theologies* (Maryknoll, NY: Orbis Books, 1985), 20, 21.

14. John Macquarrie, *Guide To The Sacraments* (New York: Continuum, 1998), 1.

15. *Communio et Progressio* (Pastoral Instruction for the Application of the Decree of the Second Vatican Ecumenical Council on the Means of Social Communication), no. 2, Pontifical Commission for the Means of Social Communication, May 23, 1971.

16. Karl Rahner, "Priest and Poet," *Theological Investigations* 3, trans. Karl-H. Kruger (Baltimore: Helicon, 1967), 298.

264.0028
C9536 LINCOLN CHRISTIAN COLLEGE AND SEMINARY

118101

3 4711 00180 5052